MATTERHORN CENTENARY

Some Works on The Alps by Sir Arnold Lunn

A CENTURY OF MOUNTAINEERING
THE SWISS AND THEIR MOUNTAINS
THE MOUNTAINS OF YOUTH
MOUNTAIN JUBILEE
MOUNTAINS OF MEMORY
SWITZERLAND AND THE ENGLISH
A HISTORY OF SKI-ING
ALPINE SKI-ING AT ALL HEIGHTS AND SEASONS
THE CRADLE OF SWITZERLAND
THE BERNESE OBERLAND
ZERMATT AND THE VALAIS

The Matterhorn at Sunrise,
from a painting by Albert Gos in the
possession of Herr Karl Weber, Zurich

Matterhorn Centenary

BY
ARNOLD LUNN

RAND McNALLY & COMPANY
CHICAGO · NEW YORK · SAN FRANCISCO

RAND McNALLY & COMPANY EDITION
PUBLISHED IN THE UNITED STATES AND
POSSESSIONS IN 1965

© *George Allen & Unwin Ltd 1965*

Library of Congress Catalog Card Number : 65-23452

PRINTED IN GREAT BRITAIN

Καὶ τόδε φωκυλίδεω· πόλις ἐν σκοπέλῳ κατὰ κόσμον
οἰκεῦσα σμικρὴ κρέσσων Νίνου ἀφραινούσης.

Thus said Phocylides: A little well-ordered city set upon
a rock is better than a frenzied Nineveh.

Phocylides — fl. 544 B.C.

CONTENTS

ILLUSTRATIONS

PREFACE

I am greatly indebted to all who helped me to obtain the necessary information and illustrations for this book, and above all to Herr Karl Weber but for whose generosity it would have been impossible to have included so many illustrations without greatly adding to the price at which the book is published.

ARNOLD LUNN

CHAPTER I

Why Men Climb

The ascent of the Matterhorn on July 14, 1865, marked the end of an epoch, the so-called 'Golden Age of Mountaineering', for the Matterhorn was the last of the Swiss four-thousand-metre peaks to be climbed.

Mountain travel is as old as man, but it was not until the nineteenth century that mountaineering was recognized as a sport. Prior to the nineteenth century, the occasional ascent of a big peak was only an isolated stunt, as for instance the first ascent of Mont Aiguille near Grenoble, which is still considered a moderately difficult peak, and which was first climbed during the year when Columbus discovered America, for it was in 1492 that King Charles VIII of France commanded his unfortunate chamberlain, de Beaupré, to climb Mont Aiguille (6,880 feet above the sea). Even today fixed ropes are attached to the trickier passages on this climb, so it is not surprising that de Beaupré only succeeded thanks to 'subtle means and engines'.

No true mountaineer could be content with a single climb, but none of those who made the rare first ascents of the eighteenth century, the conquerors, for instance, of Titlis, Buet, Vélan or Dent du Midi, ever made a second virgin climb. Not even the ascent of Mont Blanc in 1786 by the local Chamonix doctor, Michel Paccard, and Jacques Balmat had much influence on the development of mountaineering as a sport.

In his introduction to the Lonsdale Library volume on mountaineering Professor T. Graham Brown, F.R.S., describes the eccentric Benedictine monk, Father Placidus à Spescha, as 'perhaps the first of the true mountaineers'. Between 1788 and 1824 Father Placidus, who certainly did not belong to the 'one man—one mountain' school, made nine first ascents and took

15

part in the first ascent of the Tödi though only his companions reached the actual summit.[1]

Outstanding among the pioneers of authentic mountaineering were the Meyers, a Swiss family of prosperous Aarau merchants, their most remarkable achievement being the first ascent of the Jungfrau in 1811. By the middle of the nineteenth century the Swiss mountaineers had by far the best record, their virgin ascents including the Finsteraarhorn, Jungfrau, Wetterhorn (Hasli Jungfrau peak), the Piz Bernina, the Vélan, the Tödi, the Dent du Midi and the Titlis, but within a few years the initiative had passed from the Swiss to the British. Of the thirty-nine major peaks first ascended during the 'Golden Age of Mountaineering', which is generally regarded as beginning in 1854 and ending in 1865, thirty-one were first ascended by British amateurs with, of course, local guides, mostly Swiss.

As this book will be read not only by mountaineers but also, I hope, by some of the many thousand non-mountaineering visitors to Switzerland, may I attempt for their benefit to interpret the motives which induce men to climb?

If a mountaineer only climbed to enjoy the view from the summit, Ruskin would have made a valid point when he maintained that 'the real glory of the Alps is to be seen, and only to be seen, where all may see it, the child, the cripple and the man with grey hairs'. I would agree that the view of the Jungfrau from the Wengernalp is more beautiful than the view from the summit of the Jungfrau, but I am glad to have seen both views, for there is no aspect of the mountains which is not precious to the mountain lover. Moreover, the educated eye of the mountaineer discovers a beauty in mountains as seen from the plains which is unperceived by those who have never climbed. Ruskin saw far more in 'the Stones of Venice' than a casual tripper with no interest in architecture, and the mountaineer sees far more in a mountain than Ruskin ever saw. *L'amore di qualunque cosa è figliulo d'essa cognitione. L'amore è tanto piu fervente, quanto la cognitione è piu certa.* Leonardo's great saying is certainly true of mountains. 'The love of a thing is the daughter of know-

[1] I have summarized the early history of mountaineering in my book *A Century of Mountaineering*, and Father Placidus's climbs in *The Swiss and their Mountains*. Both books were supported by the Swiss Foundation for Alpine Research and published by Messrs. George Allen & Unwin Ltd.

The Matterhorn (1849) by John Ruskin

[reproduced from *Modern Painter*

3. The Cervin, from the north-west, by John Ruskin

ledge, and the love is more fervent when the knowledge is more profound.'

The mountain which one has climbed has spells which enable one 'to beget the golden time again'. It is enriched with remembered beauty and remembered adventure. Indeed, the chief reward of the mountaineer is not the view from the summit of a great peak but the view of the same peak from the valley.

Primarily, of course, one climbs a difficult mountain for the fun of climbing. Mountaineering is a sport, and the essence of sport is the invention of an *artificial* problem for the fun of solving it. A modern sportsman does not shoot pheasants because he is hungry; he preserves game for the pleasure of shooting. The contrast between mountain travel and mountaineering is similar to the contrast between hunting for food and hunting for fun. Primitive man crossed mountain passes to get to the other side. Even glacier passes were crossed in our era. Roman coins, for instance, have been found on the Théodule which links Zermatt and Breuil.

In 1574 Josias Simler, a professor at Zürich, published a book of practical advice on mountain travel above the snow-line. He understood the use of the rope, crampons, dark spectacles, and paper as a protection against cold, and much that he has to say about avalanches and crevasses is very sound, but he was writing for travellers who were *forced* to cross the Alps and had no more affection for mountains than sea-sick travellers for the Straits of Dover. That great mountaineer, A. F. Mummery, on the other hand, was writing for mountaineers who crossed passes for the fun of crossing them. 'My attention', he wrote, 'was riveted by the Col du Lion and it was brought to my mind that no more circuitous or inconvenient method of getting from Zermatt to Breuil could possibly be devised than by using this same col as a pass.' And so he crossed it.

Our verdict on a particular sport is necessarily influenced by the value which we attach to the qualities which it tests. Mountaineering is a many-sided sport, for the expert must master the techniques of rock-climbing, step-cutting in ice, and route-finding in all conditions of weather. It is fascinating to watch a master cragsman gliding up a rock face without apparent effort. He seldom seems to search for a foothold, and when he stretches

B

forth his hands they seldom come empty away. From chance irregularities he evokes a harmony of co-ordinated and uninterrupted movement. Not only rock but ice demands delicate balance, particularly if step-cutting has been reduced to a minimum by the skilful use of crampons. The expert step-cutter and the scratch golfer have at least one thing in common, a talent for striking a particular object with great accuracy and at exactly the right angle. Anybody can knock a golf ball round a golf course, and anybody can cut some sort of a step in ice, but the iceman, like the golfer, is judged by the number of strokes which he requires to achieve his object.

To be a master of one's medium is profoundly satisfying whatever that medium may be—the keys, for instance, which the great pianist strikes with unerring accuracy, or the chance irregularities of a rock face which the cragsman exploits, but the climber's mastery of his medium is, in one respect at least, more exciting than the pianist's, for if the pianist strikes a wrong note he suffers a momentary aesthetic distress, but the climber's first serious mistake may also be his last. Not that mountaineers court danger for its own sake. No mountaineer is happy leading a rock climb where the margin of safety has been unjustifiably reduced, and where he knows that he is in real danger of coming off. What the rock-climber really enjoys is the contrast between great *apparent* danger and his own conviction of complete security, an enjoyment recaptured by Geoffrey Winthrop Young in the lines,

> In this short span
> Between my finger tips and the smooth edge
> And these tense feet cramped to a crystal ledge
> I hold the life of man.

Perhaps the deepest satisfaction of the mountaineer derives not from the skilful exploitation, as in rock-climbing, of the ingenious mechanism of the human body, but from the intellectual satisfaction of mastering the craft of route-finding. There are indeed few experiences in the mountains more satisfying than to lead a guideless party in a storm to shelter and safety by the correct interpretation of small clues whose significance is only apparent to a master of mountain craft.

My only object in writing this brief and, I fear, in the main unconvincing apologia for mountaineering is to render a little less unintelligible to the non-mountaineering reader of this book the motives of the men whose adventures on the Matterhorn will be described in the chapters which follow.

NOTE

'*Something familiar about it.*' The contrast discussed in this chapter between mountain travel and mountaineering may be illustrated by Julien Hall's vivid description of his escape during the second world war from Italy into Switzerland. There was only one way of doing it, he was told. 'You must cross the Felik-Joch. The other and easier passes are guarded by the Germans: *è lunga, è faticosa, ma è più sicura: avanti!*'

A guide accompanied the thirteen prisoners of war. They called him Goliath. Goliath 'was out to beat the Germans as much as to help the British. If we were caught, for us it was Germany; but for him and his friend it was death.' Goliath and his friend left them on the pass. 'As Italians they dared not enter Switzerland, where they would have been interned. We had nothing to do but descend at our leisure. We were free, we needed no guide, said Goliath.

'How wrong he was we were yet to discover. In order to come down from the Felik-Joch one has to negotiate a glacier which is among the most dangerous in Switzerland: so we were told by the Swiss troops who came out to look for us that afternoon. By them we were taken to the Bétemps hut. It was an arduous descent: we marvelled at the dangers and at the skill of the Swiss. But it was mechanical work. We were safe: the Germans could not touch us: we had crossed the Pass. Neither for the body nor for the spirit was it an adventure, a living experience, as the night and morning had been.

'Walking down to Zermatt on the following day, I learned the names of the mountains which had formed our anonymous world. There was Monte Rosa, and Castor and Pollux, and the Breithorn—the inns at Champeluc had been called after them. They had meaning for me now. They were skeletons still, but the flesh of my own life covered them, the blood of my own memories was coursing through their stony veins.

'And I made one discovery more important than all the rest. A single peak had something familiar about it. Either I remembered it from photographs and sketches, or else its shape has a symmetry which sets it apart from that monstrous family and lends to it an artistic perfection. It was, I learned, Mont Cervin (or Monte Cervino), and Mont Cervin and the Matterhorn are one and the same peak. It was the Matterhorn which had looked at me that morning with the rosy pink glow on its cheek.'

My quotation is from a very vivid description of his adventure which Mr Julien Hall contributed to the *British Ski Year Book* for 1948.

CHAPTER II

Matterhorn Names

Passes have always been important, but it is only in comparatively modern times that men have taken much interest in peaks.
Uncounted thousands have been compelled to cross passes
because a particular pass was the shortest route to their destina-
tion. Fortresses have been built and battles have been fought on
passes, but nobody was compelled to climb a peak. It was not
indeed until the end of the eighteenth century that men began
to be interested in peaks.

Prior to the nineteenth century many passes were named, but
most peaks now famous were still anonymous. Thus, for the
natives of the Valtournanche, the Matterhorn, which dominated
their valley, was just 'The Big Rock', and to this day the Matterhorn in the valley dialect is still called 'La Grand' Becca'. Because
passes were named long before peaks, the Italian name of the
Matterhorn, Cervino, is a corruption of a name first applied to
the Théodule pass.

I am indebted for this fact, and for most of the facts in this
chapter to a Swiss, Dr Jules Guex, who has written with outstanding distinction on Alpine nomenclature. I have seldom read
a contribution to an Alpine periodical which impressed me more
than Dr Guex's article 'Cervin o Servin' in *Die Alpen*, the
journal of the Swiss Alpine Club.[1]

As late as the sixteenth century, Dr Guex assures us, map-
makers and geographical writers never mention the Matterhorn
by name, but often refer to the pass which we call St Théodule,
and which was almost certainly crossed in Roman times. Dr
Guex gives a list of the fourteen names by which St Théodule
pass has been called at various times. Of these names for the St

[1] (1940-1941, pp. 147-150).

Théodule, Mont Servin (1560-1855) began as the name of the
Théodule pass and ended in a corrupt form, Cervin, as the name
of the Matterhorn itself.

The name Mons Silvius for the Théodule pass makes its first
appearance in the writings of Gilles Tschudi who informs us that
the Mons Silvius, though a glacier pass, can be crossed without
danger in summer either on foot or on muleback. In 1574 Professor Josias Simler adopted Tschudi's name, Mons Silvius, for
the Théodule, and in 1904 the Rev. W. A. B. Coolidge, who was
one of the greatest Alpine authorities in his day, improved on
Tschudi by suggesting that Mons Silvius was probably the
original name of the Matterhorn.

Dr Guex has no patience with all this guess work. There is no
evidence that Mons Silvius is anything but the invention of
Tschudi. There is no document, Latin or medieval, in which
the Théodule is referred to as Mons Silvius, and no evidence that
the Théodule was ever known as Mons Silvius by the natives of
Zermatt or the Valtournanche. The name Mons Silvius is the
by-product of classical snobbery. Those whom Dr Guex rather
unkindly describes as the 'snobs of humanism' were always
happy if they could discover a classical origin for a place name
or a tradition, and were not always too exacting in their demand
for evidence. They themselves frequently latinized both personal
and geographical names. Thus Gilles Tschudi insisted on being
called Aegidius Scudus and Simler signed himself Simlerus. It is
to Simler that we are indebted for such absurdities as Mons
Letschius for the Lötschen pass and Mons Piniferus for the German Fichtelgebirge. Simler not only adopted Tschudi's Mons
Silvius but explained this fictitious name, for which Tschudi
alone is responsible, as the name of a Roman General Silvius for
whose existence Simler is our only authority.

The name Mont Servin, originally applied to the Théodule,
makes its first appearance in a document dated 1560, in which
the inhabitants of Avas and of Brusson (Valle di Challant)
petitioned the Consiglio dei Commissari of Aosta for permission
to construct fortifications on their alps. In this document we find
these words: 'Au cousté de Montservin, soyt Royse, il y a un
libre passage pour les chevaulx at aultres bêtes et gens'.

Royse, La Roèse, Roise and Rosa are all variants of a word

which we should translate 'glacier'. Monte Rosa is merely Valtournanche for 'the Glacier Mountain', and does not take its name from the rose of dawn on the snows of the peak. If *rosa* meant rosy or red, the Pointe de Rosa Blanche near the Combin (Point of Rosy White) would be self-contradictory as a name.

Dr Guex traces the word Servinus from *silva*, a wood. In the Alps the Latin word *silva* gradually became corrupted. *Silva* evolved through *selva*, *selve* and later *serva* and *serve*. The word retained through all transformations the original meaning, 'wood'. Even today the Savoyards in their dialect use the word *serve*. In the Savoy Alps and in Piedmont many place names are corruptions of *silva*, as, for instance, La Serve, Le Servet (the small wood), Tresserve (beyond the wood), and La Servage (the woody place). Mont Servin, as the name of a mountain, occurs four times in the Alps—in the commune of Puygros, Savoy, above Balme in the valley of Lanzo, in the Valle d'Angrone, and finally as an early name of the Matterhorn. The name Mont Servin conveys the idea of a peak whose slopes are covered with woods.

At the beginning of the seventeenth century, or perhaps before, the Valaisians erected on the Col du Mont Servin a chapel or an oratory named after the patron of the pass, Theodulus, first Bishop of Octodurum (Martigny) in the fourth century. The name Col St Théodule in time replaced Mont Servin just as the Grand St Bernard replaced Mont Joux, and St Bernardin replaced Monte Uccello. But, as Dr Guex remarks, the name Mont Servin had more survival value than Mont Joux or Monte Uccello. Indeed, so far from disappearing, it received promotion, and Mont Servin, which began as the name of a pass. ended gloriously as the name of the Matterhorn. In 1680 Tommaso Borgonio, an Italian, published a map of the Duchy of Savoy, and bestowed on the highest point in the Duchy the name M. Servino. A hundred years later, in 1786, Nicola de Robilant, in his *Essai géographique* (Turin), p. 183, makes the first literary allusion to the Matterhorn at Mont Servin.

It was Horace Bénédict de Saussure, the distinguished Genevese scientist who climbed Mont Blanc in 1787, who was responsible for the modern name, Cervin. On August 14, 1789, he crossed the St Théodule from Breuil to Zermatt and described the journey in his *Voyages dans les Alpes*. The view from the Théodule made a profound impression on him, particularly 'the great and superb pyramid of Mont-Cervin which rises to an immense height in the form of a triangular obelisk of living rock, and which has the appearance of being carved by a chisel'.

Mont Servin was, so Dr Guex assures us, only one of many local names which de Saussure had mutilated, but of his orthographical blunders Mont Cervin was the most disastrous. Such was his immense prestige that the correct form disappeared and was replaced by Cervin. Dr Guex's rejection of Cervin was the more convincing because the romantic derivation of the name from *cerf* (stag) would, if correct, be one of the very rare exceptions to the general rule that the inhabitants of mountain valleys, the *Berglers*, showed little imagination in naming mountains. The Jungfrau, so called not because it was a virgin peak, for at that time all peaks were virgin, but because of the convent of *Jungfrauen* at the foot of the Jungfrau, and the Mönch next to the Jungfrau, are among the few exceptions which I can recall to the unromantic nomenclature of *Berglers*. Thus there are in the Alps innumerable white, black and red peaks (Mont Blanc, Weisshorn, Dent Blanche, Schwarzhorn, Rothorn, Monte Nero, Dent Rouge, Monterosso), many peaks which take their name from the fact that they served as primitive sundials (Dent du Midi, Mittaghorn) and of course many broad peaks (Lauterbrunnen Breithorn, Zermatt Breithorn), but it is to mountaineers that we are indebted for almost all the romantic names such as the Dent du Requin, the Adler pass and the Col des Hirondelles.

CHAPTER III

Early Visitors to Zermatt

The first documentary reference to the valley of Zermatt, dated 1218, records the sale of tithes and is witnessed by the *major* of Chousont, the modern St Niklaus, a village half way between Visp and Zermatt, the birthplace of Joseph Knubel and Franz Lochmatter, two of the greatest guides in Alpine history. The *majors* in the thirteenth century were hereditary officials who acted as magistrates, and the *majories* were confined to important places. It is therefore clear that even in the thirteenth century St Niklaus had established itself as a village of some standing. By the end of the thirteenth century there was a church and resident priest at Zermatt, for in a document dated 1280 one of the witnesses was the priest of Zermatt, Waltherus, Curatus de Pratoborno.

Pratoborno, the old name of the valley, is a compound of two words, *Pratum* and *Bornum*. Pratum is a latinized form of the German word *Matte*, a meadow. Many explanations have been suggested for *Bornum*, and of these Dr Albert Julen's[1] appears to me the most probable. *Borgne* in the dialect of French Switzerland may mean a boundary but can also mean a spring or river, i.e. Borgne von Evolène. In the Middle Ages the feudal lords who exercised jurisdiction in the valley were French-speaking, and Pratobornium (Praborgne) probably meant the meadow in the region in which the rivers spring (*Matte im Quellgebiet*). The German name can be traced back to the end of the fifteenth century in the form *Matt*. In the same century the Théodule was often called the Passus Pratoborni or Matterberg (later Matterjoch). *Matt* evolved into *Die Matt, von der Matt, Zur Matt*, the modern form Zermatt finding universal adoption not earlier

[1] *Die Namen von Zermatt und seinem Bergen im Lichte der Geschichte.*

24

than the middle of the nineteenth century. The Matterhorn, the peak of the meadows, is a striking example of the general rule that mountain people showed little imagination in naming mountains. The name 'Zermatt' first appears on a map of the Valais in the year 1682. The oldest house in the village has inside it the date A.D. 1539. In 1538 115 families purchased their freedom from their feudal lords of the Rhone valley, and by 1618 there were 182 families who had earned the right to call themselves free citizens. In 1540 the first free parish was established with its own parish church, and a magistrate and judge elected by the people.

On Christmas Day 1618, after the last group of subject families had bought their freedom, the village was pronounced 'closed' and the *bourgeoisie*, for which the German equivalent, *Burgerschaft*, soon came into use, came into existence.

The Swiss are proud of their democratic constitution but Swiss mountain valleys are an engaging blend of oligarchy and democracy. The *Burgerschaft*, which at one time was general throughout Switzerland, now only retains its original form in some of the mountain valleys, and in these the *Burgerschaft* is perhaps the most exclusive aristocracy in Europe.

There are only twenty families on the roll of the present Zermatt *Burgerschaft*. The following twenty-one names are those of the families which constituted the original membership: Aufdenblatten, Biner, Brantschen, Furrer, Graven, Inderbinen, Julen, Kronig, Lauber, Moser, Perren, Ruden, Salzgeber, Schuler, Siegrist, Taugwalder, Welschen, Zmut, Zumtaugwald and Zurniven.

Only one family has been admitted to the exclusive oligarchy since it was first founded, the Seilers, and then only as the result of an eighteen years' battle and the direct intervention of the Cantonal Government.[1]

All residents of Zermatt belong to the 'political commune', whether they are or are not members of the *Burgerschaft*, and it is their elected representatives who are in control of the commune. The *Burgerschaft* is a private corporation which owns

[1] The story of this struggle is told in Dr Kämpfer's book *Ein Burgerrechtsstreit im Wallis* and is summarized in my book *Zermatt and the Valais*, pp. 22-3.

everything which is not private property, the forests, streams, glaciers and even the mountains. The Swiss summit of the Matterhorn and the north, east and west faces belong to the *Burgerschaft*.

The *Burgerschaft* owns a great deal of land, electric power and water installations, various ski-lifts and the Hotel Zermatterhof, a first-class hotel, admirably run. The income from all this property is divided among the families of the *Burgerschaft*, all of whom are expected to contribute in money or in labour to any new project. When the Zermatterhof was being built in 1877, most members took part in the manual labour of construction, and only those who could produce very good reasons were allowed to make instead a cash contribution.

The climate of Zermatt has changed radically since the middle of the eighteenth century, when the alpine pastures of Zermatt and the Valtournanche met on the Théodule and a bridle path led from Zermatt to Breuil.

The first visitor to Zermatt to leave on record a detailed description of the region was Gilles Tschudi, the founder of Swiss historical research. He crossed the Théodule to Zermatt in 1524 and described the valley in *Die uralt wahrhaftig alpisch Rhetia*, which was published in 1538 and included a map of the Valais. Professional guides could be hired at Zermatt as far back as the sixteenth century, a fact which is mentioned by Josias Simler in the first book ever to give practical advice on mountain travel above the snow-line.

The first traveller to have left a fairly detailed description of a visit to Zermatt was the Swiss botanist, Abraham Thomas, who stayed there in 1765. The Zermatters were convinced that these strangers were spies whose task was to reconnoitre the passes, and then to steal sheep on the higher pasturages and drive them across the Théodule. A mob assembled outside the curé's house where the botanists were staying, and the curé had great difficulty in pacifying them. Abraham Thomas, uninfluenced by his reception at Zermatt, described the Zermatters as 'simple, hard-working, religious, hospitable and faithful but mistrustful where strangers are concerned. I should advise travellers first to make the acquaintance of the curé.'

In 1789 de Saussure crossed the Théodule with a convoy of

mules, which would certainly not be practicable today. In his description of the view from the summit he singles out for special praise the Cervin, this being, I believe, the first instance of the misspelling of the name Servin, an error which was to be perpetuated, an unfortunate result of de Saussure's immense prestige. The curé, who had not forgotten the hostile reception of the botanists, flatly refused to offer de Saussure hospitality, but 'a kind of innkeeper' was finally prevailed on to provide some kind of hospitality.

George Cade, of York, who crossed the Théodule to Zermatt in 1800, was the first Englishman to visit Zermatt. The curé, who was very friendly, sent him a message that 'he would wish for nothing so much as to be of service'. They spent the evening together and the curé described the horrors of the French invasion. 'When the enemy reached Zermatt', wrote Cade, 'the same cruelties were repeated with an extortion of 500,000 livres. Meanwhile our host, this excellent old man, was bound, and a poignard held at his breast till the demand was exacted. The brave and generous villagers sacrificed everything for their priest.'

In the 1830s, most of the visitors to Zermatt stayed with the local doctor, Dr Lauber, among them Sir John Herschel in 1821 and William Brockedon, the English painter, in 1825. In 1830 Lord Minto and his sixteen-year-old son with seven Chamonix guides arrived in Zermatt, and climbed the Breithorn in spite of the protests of the Zermatters against taking a boy of sixteen on such a dangerous climb.

Among the early Swiss visitors may be mentioned Dr Samuel Brunner of Berne and the Bernese geologist Studer who made a long stay at the curé's house where the party were charged a franc and a half a day including wine. In 1839 Dr Lauber obtained the right to change his chalet into a hotel, which was named Hotel Cervie and later Monte Rose. It had only three beds and accommodated not more than about a dozen travellers a year. The first visitors to the Monte Rose in 1839 were the Swiss scientists, Desor, Agassiz and Studer.

In 1844 John Ruskin paid his first visit to Zermatt. He was fascinated by the Matterhorn and hardly mentions the Weisshorn or Zinal Rothorn. He was the first to photograph the

Matterhorn, 'The first sun-portrait ever taken of the Matterhorn —and as far as I know of any Swiss mountain', he wrote in *Deucalion*, 'was taken by me in the year 1849'. In those early days photography was a difficult art, and on his second visit to Zermatt, Ruskin brought with him a complete laboratory and produced some really beautiful prints. And perhaps because he had taken all this trouble to produce a 'sun portrait' of the great peak, his own painting of it, which I reproduce in this book, was perhaps the first painting with no distortion of ridge or face.

Ruskin was also the first to find words worthy of his theme in the long passage in which he evokes the majesty of the great peak. Here is one paragraph from the passage in question, which will be found in *The Stones of Venice*[1]:

'It has been falsely represented as a peak or tower. It is a vast ridged promontory, connected at its western root with the Dent d'Erin, and lifting itself like a rearing horse with its face to the east. All the way along the flank of it, for half a day's journey on the Zmutt glacier, the grim black terraces of its foundations range almost without a break; and the clouds, when their day's work is done, and they are weary, lay themselves down on those foundation steps, and rest till dawn, each with his leagues of grey mantle stretched along the grisly ledge, and the cornice of the mighty wall gleaming in the moonlight, three thousand feet above.'

Ruskin worshipped mountains and regarded mountaineers as vandals desecrating the cathedrals of Nature. 'The Alps themselves,' he wrote, 'which your own poets used to love so reverently, you look upon as soaped poles in a bear garden, which you set yourself to climb and slide down again with "shrieks of delight". When you are past shrieking, having no human articulate voice to say you are glad with, you fill the quietude of their valleys with gunpowder blasts, and rush home, red with the cutaneous eruption of conceit, and voluble with the convulsive hiccough of self-satisfaction.'

It would be impossible to conceive a more grotesque travesty of the attitude of those dignified gentlemen, the leading pioneers; Leslie Stephen, for instance, or Mr Justice Wills, or Charles

[1] Vol. 1, ch. 5.

Matthews. Many of these pioneers went out of their way to give the main credit for their successes to their guides, and conceit was not a noticeable failing in Alpine Club members. Ruskin's outburst was, I suspect, influenced by an unconscious jealousy of those who had done what he would have been proud to do. Mountaineering is an ascetic sport, and the mountaineer may well have reinforced Ruskin's recurring suspicion that the quality of his own life would have been improved by an ascetic element. 'He was a man', writes Mr Wilenski in an admirable biography,[1] 'who, it seems to me, had only one fault in his character—self-indulgence. . . . But his self-indulgence was a definite weakness in his character.' As indeed Ruskin himself realized. 'You fed me effeminately', he wrote to his father, 'and luxuriously to that extent that I actually now could not travel in rough countries without taking a cook with me.'

Ruskin was not only conscious of his own self-indulgence, which effectively prevented him from crossing the boundary which separates mountain rambling from mountaineering, but he realized the educative effect of danger. 'That question of the moral effect of danger', he wrote to his father from Chamonix in 1863, 'is a very curious one; but this I know and find, practically, that if you come to a dangerous place, and turn back from it, though it may have been perfectly right and wise to do so, still your *character* has suffered some slight deterioration; you are to that extent weaker, more lifeless, more effeminate, more liable to passion and error in future; whereas if you go through with the danger, though it may have been apparently wrong and foolish to encounter it, you come out of the encounter a stronger and better man, fitter for every sort of work and trial, and *nothing but danger* produces this effect.' And perhaps the fact that he never did 'go through with the danger' explains the venom with which he attacked those who did.

Later he relented. 'No blame,' he wrote in the second edition of *Sesame and Lilies*, which was published shortly after the Matterhorn accident, 'ought to attach to the Alpine tourist for incurring danger . . . some experience of distinct peril, and the acquirements of habits of quick and calm action in its presence, are necessary elements at some period of life in the formation of

[1] *John Ruskin*, p. 36.

manly character.' In 1866 he was induced by a friend to attend the winter dinner of the Alpine Club. 'He declined to speak,' writes Leslie Stephen, 'and at first looked at us as rather questionable characters, but rapidly thawed, and became not only courteous, but cordially appreciative of our motives. I think he called us "fine young men".'

Shortly after the dinner he joined the club on a literary qualification and remained a member for many years.

In 1854 a new hotel, the Mont Cervin, was opened on the same site as the modern Hotel Mont Cervin, but the most important event in the development of Zermatt as a tourist centre was the acquisition by Alexander Seiler of Dr Lauber's inn, the Monte Rose, which was renamed the Hotel Monte Rosa.

In conclusion let me cordially commend *Zermatt Saga* by Cicely Williams, wife of the Bishop of Leicester, an admirable study not only of Zermatt but also of the Zermatters. Mrs Williams is a keen mountaineer and skier with a gift, which only a minority of mountaineers possess, of encouraging the *Berglers* to talk to her not only as a climber but also as a friend.

CHAPTER IV

Alexander Seiler and the Development of Zermatt

No man made a greater contribution to the development of Zermatt as a tourist centre than Alexander Seiler, who took over Lauber's Inn, the Hotel Monte Rose, and renamed it the Hotel Monte Rosa.

Alexander Seiler was born in 1819 in Blitzingen in the Upper Rhone valley, a few miles from Niederwald, the birthplace of another prince of hoteliers, César Ritz.

Seiler served an apprenticeship to a soap manufacturer and then settled down in Sion, prepared to buy or sell anything which was the first stage in a business career.

Meanwhile his brother Joseph, who had been appointed curate in Zermatt, conveyed to Alexander a proposal by the parish priest that Alexander should help build a hotel on the Riffelalp. The parish priest would put up half the money if the brothers Seiler would subscribe the remaining half. It was actually not until 1884 that Joseph Seiler's first proposal was carried into effect and the Riffelalp hotel opened under the direction of the Seilers, but in 1855 Alexander Seiler acquired Lauber's Inn which was destined, as the Hotel Monte Rosa, to become the most famous mountaineering hotel in the Alps, and the unchallenged headquarters of the Alpine Club.

'We have with us to-night,' said Captain J. P. Farrar at a meeting of the Alpine Club of which he was President from 1917 to 1919, 'Herr Joseph Seiler, grandson of Alexander Seiler, the creator of Zermatt. Few indeed are the Prime Ministers of England whose memory is held in such high esteem by members of this club as that of Alexander Seiler.'

'Seiler', wrote Cicely Williams in a charming article which she contributed to *Chamber's Journal*,[1] 'was the hotelier *par excellence*. He understood exactly the art of innkeeping. He knew just how to cater for the comfort of the mountaineer; how to welcome arriving guests, thirsting for more conquests; how to bid farewell to the successful and the disappointed. No one was merely a room number to Seiler—each visitor was his personal guest. He entertained them to wine and always sat at the head of the long dining-table, he himself giving the sign for the beginning and ending of the meal.'

Though the hotel, which is still owned by the Seiler family, has been expanded and modernized, its external appearance is little changed from Whymper's day, and the remains of the original inn are just to the left of the main entrance.

Alexander Seiler owed much of his success to his remarkable wife, Katharina Cathrein, the descendant of Austrians who migrated from Tirol to the Valais in the middle of the eighteenth century. She was the mother of sixteen children and found time not only to look after her large family and to help in the administration of the hotel, but also to make a great contribution in time and money to works of charity. Facing the Mont Cervin Hotel is the garden belonging to the hotel, which contains a monument to Alexander Seiler and his wife.

The Zermatt Museum in the garden is now under the direction of Herr Karl Lehner. It contains splendid reliefs of the Matterhorn and Monte Rosa groups, photographs of Alpine pioneers, old prints of Zermatt, and many mountaineering relics, among them the three ropes used on the first ascent of the Matterhorn, including the weak rope which broke.

Not far away is the Monte Rosa Hotel with the medallion of Edward Whymper on the wall. Facing the Monte Rosa is the Zermatterhof, which is owned by the Burgers of Zermatt and directed by Herr Stopfer. Just beyond the Monte Rosa, on the right-hand side, is the old priest's house, little changed since the botanist, Abraham Thomas, stopped there in 1765. The Catholic church is modern, but the altar of the Sacred Heart (1720) is the work of Johan Ritz of the family which later produced the famous hotelier, César Ritz.

[1] August 1953.

4. Edward Whymper in the year of the first ascent

5. Edward Whymper in 1910, aged 70

CHAPTER V

The First Attempt

The first lighthearted attempt to discover a route to the summit of the Matterhorn was made in 1857, the year in which the Alpine Club, mother of all Alpine Clubs, was founded in London. These, the first pioneers of the Matterhorn, were men of the Valtournanche: Jean Jacques Carrel, Jean Antoine Carrel, and a young priest, Aimé Gorret.

It was the Matterhorn, as Guido Rey points out in his book, which was to create a school of great guides, and to save from mediocrity the guides who, in the intervals of smuggling, led travellers across the Théodule. It was, of course, from the ranks of smugglers that these guides came, and the travellers who employed them had often to wait some days before they could spare time from their more exacting profession.

Only a small minority of these guides felt completely secure even on the Théodule, and the dangers of 'traversing Mont Cervin' were vividly described to such travellers as were anxious to cross the pass to Zermatt. No guide would have crossed the pass without a second guide to divide the responsibility, for the traveller William Brockedon had to wait two days and two nights until his guide, Jean Baptiste Pession, could procure a second guide.

'To the men of Valtournanche,' writes Guido Rey, 'all strangers, even German and French, were Englishmen. Quintino Sella himself, when he climbed the Breithorn in 1854, did not escape being taken for an Englishman.' 'Fortunately for us,' writes Gorret, 'he was an Englishman from Biella.'

The Théodule guides were far from competent. They had not even mastered the use of the rope, and certainly in the 'forties the Zermatt guides were no better. Peter Damatter, who guided

J. D. Forbes from Zermatt across the Théodule, carried neither rope nor axe, nor even a sharp pointed stick—nothing but an umbrella.

Mont Blanc was first climbed in 1786, and various ascents were made in the first half of the nineteenth century. For this reason, the standard of guiding was far higher in Chamonix than in the Valtournanche, and Chamonix guides on their way through the Valtournanche often hired the local guides to carry their luggage. They preferred them to the Zermatters because they spoke the same language, the Valtournanche being French-speaking, and perhaps because they were less exacting in the matter of wages. The Valtourneins, however, were not long content with their role as mere porters to the Chamoniards. They benefited from these contacts with first-class guides and learned how to behave to travellers. Before long there were a number of guides who made a practice of waiting for possible clients at Châtillon, clients whom they would then guide across the Théodule and, more rarely, across the Col des Cimes Blanches, but it was some time before they succeeded in living down their old reputation. The 1854 edition of Murray's Handbook, for instance, warns travellers that 'the Châtillon guides are not trustworthy', and to Edward Whymper, the Valtournanche guides represented 'pointers out of paths, and large consumers of meat and drink but little more'. Whymper revised a verdict which did not err on the side of charity when he climbed with Jean Antoine Carrel.

Even in the 'fifties there were some good guides in the Valtournanche; Pierre and Charles Emmanuel Gorret, for instance, who were described as excellent guides by that great English pioneer, Alfred Wills. But none of them showed the slightest interest in the Matterhorn.

Canon Carrel of Aosta, who was a son of the Valtournanche, was almost certainly the first of the Valtourneins to consider the possibility of climbing Mont Cervin, and to speculate on the increase in material prosperity which would result if the Cervin attracted not only travellers to admire the great peak from the lower levels but also mountaineers to employ guides to lead them to the summit. The Canon was a man of science with a taste for research. He collected mountain flowers, and brought back from his wanderings fragments of rock of possible interest to geologists. He made many mountain excursions with men of science such as Forbes, Sismondi and Studer, and set up a small observatory on the roof of his house in 1840. He was a great reader, and familiar with the literary tributes to the Cervin from the pens of earlier travellers, and had read with keen interest the narratives of mountaineers, in particular those of the early attempts on Monte Rosa. The Canon's reputation as an authority on the valley and its mountains was such that many English visitors consulted him, with the result that he was often called 'the friend of the English'. It was perhaps because of the great interest which the Cervin provoked in these English travellers that the Canon was the first to realize what the Cervin might mean for the Valtourneins.

The three young Valtourneins who set out that morning in 1857 to explore the Italian ridge of the Cervin were all related to the Canon, and had certainly been influenced by his great interest in the peak. The oldest of this trio, Jean Jacques Carrel, was renowned as a hunter. He was a man of enterprise and courage, the only member of a search party who dared to descend on a rope into a crevasse and pull out a victim who had fallen in. Jean Antoine Carrel, destined to play a leading role in the Matterhorn drama, was a man of thirty, a discharged soldier who had fought at Novara.

The third of these climbers, Aimé Gorret, was a talented young man, a brilliant conversationalist and a gifted writer. As a seminarist he had attracted the attention of his superiors, and he was still a student when he was appointed professor at a minor seminary. He was one of Nature's nonconformists, highly unconventional and outspoken in his comments on men and manners. He had both a taste and a talent for controversy, but too little prudence. His ecclesiastical superiors were only too anxious to make full use of his talents, but were worried by his imprudence and by the needless enmities which he aroused. His career in the Church was therefore undistinguished, but he was greatly revered by Italian mountaineers, and elected with acclamation as one of the earlier honorary members of the Italian Alpine Club. His unpublished Alpine writings were in the process of being collected and edited by Professor Albert Deffeyes of

Aosta who unfortunately died before the book was ready for publication. It is to be hoped that some other editor may yet be found for writings which are of real importance in the history of mountaineering.

The Carrels and Gorret met before dawn at the chalets of Avouil above Breuil. They reached a point now known as the Tête du Lion (12,188 feet), and amused themselves by detaching big rocks and sending them thundering down the cliffs. They looked at the Matterhorn with quiet assurance. They were in no hurry; the Cervin would not run away. Sooner or later they would find a way to the summit.

Their attempt was much discussed in the valley. The general opinion, writes Rey, was that they were madmen, and that the Cervin was 'only for the English', but there were some who began to wonder whether the Cervin was as inaccessible as it seemed.

The Cervin did not run away, but a mountaineer more resolute than Carrel, an Englishman of whom nobody had heard when this first lighthearted exploration had been attempted, was to steal the great prize from the men of Valtournanche.

NOTE

I am indebted for many of the facts in this chapter to *The Matterhorn* by Guido Rey. Translated from the Italian by J. E. C. Eaton. Revised and two additional chapters by R. L. G. Irving. Basil Blackwood, Oxford, 1946.

CHAPTER VI

Edward Whymper (I)

My father and I had been invited to attend a meeting of the Alpine Club at which the late E. Russell Clarke read a paper on ski-ing, in the course of which he remarked that ski-ing had reached something like finality. The year was 1908.

'There's Whymper,' said my father. He was not the centre, as I would have expected, of a respectful group of admirers. He was alone. My father introduced me. Whymper made some banal remarks about ski-ing, and a few minutes later the lecture began.

> And did you once see Shelley plain?
> And did he stop and speak to you?

Had I really seen Whymper plain? It was difficult to realize that this dour elderly man—he was sixty-eight when we met—was the Whymper of those immortal illustrations in the first adult book which I spelt out for myself as a child, the Whymper who slid head-first down the ice slopes of the Col du Lion, who sheltered below an overhanging boulder from falling stones on the Matterhorn, and who listened to Garibaldi's followers singing the songs of the Risorgimento.

Edward Whymper was born on April 27, 1840. The Whympers were a family of Dutch origin who came over to England with William of Orange. The word *Whymper* is a corruption of the Dutch word *wimper* which means 'eye-brow'. Edward's grandfather was a brewer, his father, Josiah, a wood engraver and a painter who was elected a member of the Royal Society of Painters in Water-colours. His pupils included Frederick Walker, A.R.A., and Charles Keene, the well-known *Punch* artist. Josiah Whymper had eleven children, of whom

37

Edward was the second. His elder brother, Frederick, travelled extensively and wrote two books, *Travels in Alaska*, and *The Romance of the Sea*.

Josiah Whymper, who died at the age of ninety, and who was sufficiently well-known as an artist to be included in *Who's Who*, might have given his sons a better education had his family been less numerous. As it was, Edward was taken away from school at the age of fourteen and apprenticed to his father's wood-engraving business.

At the age of fifteen Edward Whymper began a diary, long extracts from which were published for the first time in Frank Smythe's biography.[1] The self-portrait which emerges from the pages of this diary is of a boy with strong views on a variety of subjects. The dour Calvinism of his Dutch ancestors was perhaps responsible for the youthful Whymper's fiery defence of sabbatarianism. His political prejudices were those of the Victorian middle class. He despised the proletariat and regarded the aristocracy with proper respect.

'*June 27th 1855*. Lord Robert Grosvenor last week mentioned in the House of Lords that the aristocracy were setting the commoners a better example than they had before in such matters as driving in the parks on Sunday; which speech drew forth some handbills recommending an assembly in Hyde Park to see the aforesaid good example. A number of low fellows accordingly met and saluted the nobility with cries of "don't employ y'r servants on Sunday", etc., etc., and they actually went so far as to compel the Duke and Duchess of Beaufort and several other noblemen and ladies to get out and walk, the police not interfering. This is a free country indeed when such things as these are allowed, and quickly passed over without much notice being taken of them.'

'*July 8th, 1855*. The mob . . . went down Piccadilly and in Belgrave Square breaking windows. This shows what kind of people they were. As Mr Peel said in the House, "they were mere canaille", and I quite agree with his suggestion that a few six-pounders fired into them would do a deal of good.'

[1] *Edward Whymper* by Frank Smythe. Hodder & Stoughton.

'*February* 19th 1856. Sir J. Walmsley has attempted to intro-
duce a bill (for desecrating the Sabbath really) but for Sunday
recreation as he calls it. He would have the British Museum,
National Gallery, and the Crystal Palace open on the Sunday, in
order to improve the national mind (he says) . . . It was justly
said at the meeting to-night, that for Englishmen who always
regard liberty as one of the greatest blessings, to wish to deprive
the largest body of people (the religious) *in* the country of their
privileges would be an act of the highest injustice and
oppression.'

'*December* 13th 1857. Mr C. Clark, B.A., preached both times.
Hoh! The aitches. It is perfectly 'orrible to 'ear 'eaven, 'ope,
'eart, etc. etc. For they are legion. Without this, to say the least,
Clark may be a very clever young man; but with it, I think no
man should attempt to speak in public.'

This advice Whymper himself very sensibly refused to follow,
for he was an excellent lecturer though troubled by a tendency
to drop his aitches. 'This worried him,' writes Mr Smythe, 'and
round about 1905 to 1908 he got his nephew, Mr Robert
Whymper, to attend many of his lectures and call his attention
to every omission by snapping his fingers.'
Edward's interests were those of a normal boy. He enjoyed
playing and watching cricket. 'I formed the nucleus of the North
Lambeth Cricket Club which I hope may last many years.' Above
all he was keenly interested in his work as a wood engraver.

'This block I have been engaged on for a long time past, not
so much as a specimen of my talent for *effect*, but for minuteness
and correctness of detail. I may say without vanity that in the
former of these two last I have succeeded, and have probably put
as much work in as there has ever been put in a block of the
same size before . . . The drawing was merely done as a specimen,
but on its being shown by my Father to Mr J. Murray (the
publisher) to-day, he ordered him to engrave it, as he said he
could make use of it. I hope this may be the means of bringing
my name before the public as a correct architectural draughtsman, which if I once get, I will do *my* best to keep.' (*January*
14th 1858)

It was the fact that Whymper loved his work and had mastered his chosen craft that gave him his splendid chance. His work attracted the attention of William Longman, the publisher, who was in need of somebody to illustrate a book on the Alps, and who commissioned Edward Whymper for this purpose.

Whymper was twenty years old when he crossed the Channel on July 23, 1860, on his way to Switzerland. He visited among other famous Alpine resorts, Kandersteg, Interlaken, Zermatt, Courmayeur and Chamonix. His first Alpine tour ended in the Dauphiné, for his publishers had asked him to make some sketches of Mont Pelvoux 'to celebrate the triumph of some Englishman who intended to make its ascent'. The attempt failed, and it was Whymper who was destined to make the first ascent in the following year.

Whymper's diary is more reliable as a guide to his first impressions of the Alps than anything which he wrote for the public. It was the fascination of mountain adventure rather than the appeal of mountain scenery which drew him back again and again to the Alps. He paid the conventional tributes to Alpine scenery in his famous book, *Scrambles Amongst the Alps*, but his real sentiments emerge in the diary—his disillusion, for instance, with the famous Staubbach waterfall above Lauterbrunnen: 'I had previously expected to be disappointed but felt quite sold and would not stop to look at it.'

Smythe makes an excellent point when he contrasts Whymper's first impression of the Matterhorn as recorded in his diary, with the sentiments which he put on record for the public:

'Saw, of course, the Matterhorn repeatedly; what precious stuff Ruskin has written about this, as well as about many other things. When one has a fair view of the mountain as I had, it may be compared to a sugar loaf set up on a table; the sugar loaf should have its head knocked on one side. Grand it is, but beautiful I think it is not.'

And this is what he wrote, when he was writing for the public. The quotation is from *Scrambles Amongst the Alps*: 'Ages hence generations unborn will gaze upon its awful precipices and wonder at its unique form. However exalted may be their ideas, and however exaggerated their expectations, none will come to return disappointed!'

Whymper often took great liberties with facts in order to produce a particular dramatic effect. Contrast, for instance, the description in his diary of a descent to the Gorner glacier: 'It took me three-quarters of an hour to get down 350 feet I should think. Once on the glacier, moving was pretty easy, though the crevasses at the side rendered *getting on it* a work of time to a novice,' with the long passage in *Scrambles*, more than five hundred words in length, in which the same incident is described, and which ends with a dramatic description of a jump: 'Night was approaching, and the solemn stillness of the High Alps was broken only by the sound of rushing water or of falling rocks. If the jump should be successful—well; if not, I fell into that horrible chasm, to be frozen in, or drowned in that gurgling, rushing water. Everything depended on that jump. Again I asked myself, "Can it be done?" It *must* be. So, finding my stick was useless, I threw it and the sketch-book to the ice, and first retreating as far as possible, ran forward with all my might, took the leap, barely reached the other side, and fell awkwardly on my knees. Almost at the same moment a shower of stones fell on the spot from which I had jumped.'

One of the most famous illustrations in *Scrambles* depicts Whymper's guide, Christian Almer, landing on an unstable block after jumping across a deep notch in the west ridge of the Ecrins which Whymper's party descended after making the first ascent of the Ecrins. No mountaineer who subsequently climbed or descended this ridge reported the existence of the famous notch. Many years later, the Rev. W. A. B. Coolidge, a mountaineer whose knowledge of the Alps and of Alpine history was only surpassed by his passion for Alpine controversy, remarked in the course of an obituary notice of Christian Almer that Almer denied that he had made the jump described and depicted by Whymper, a jump which Whymper's companion on the climb, A. W. Moore, never mentioned in his published account of the same expedition. Whymper demanded an Extraordinary General Meeting of the Alpine Club, whereupon Coolidge resigned from the Club.

The Alpine Club shortly afterwards elected Coolidge an

Honorary Member, an action which Whymper interpreted as indirect support for Coolidge's attack on his veracity. In 1911, the last year of his life, Whymper called on Coolidge in his Grindelwald chalet. Frank Smythe quotes a statement in Whymper's diary to the effect that he 'came to Grindelwald expressly to have an interview with the Rev. W. A. B. Coolidge, and to form an opinion, if possible, as to the state of his mind'. It is reassuring to learn that Whymper 'did not detect any signs of insanity'. The famous Ecrins jump, so Coolidge himself told me, was never referred to in the course of their conversation, perhaps because Whymper realized that nothing would have induced Coolidge to modify the statement which had provoked the controversy.

Coolidge, whose courage in written controversy tended to evaporate when confronted with the possibility of a face-to-face argument, was, I think, relieved when he parted with Whymper after a meeting which lasted from 10 a.m. to 5.15 p.m. He never belittled Whymper's mountaineering achievements, but his gloss on a certain incident described by Whymper in *Scrambles* was characteristic of Coolidge's feline malice.

'You will remember, my dear Lunn,' said the sage of Grindelwald, 'that after climbing the Ecrins, Whymper and Moore spent the night under different rocks. Whymper tells us that he left Moore because he and Croz thought they would try for a roof before finally abandoning all hope of reaching civilization. The truth is that Moore remained behind because Whymper had got on his nerves. You see, Whymper was pretty uncouth and Moore was a distinguished Civil Servant. He was a bit of a swell and Whymper grated on him.'

CHAPTER VII

Early Attempts on the Matterhorn

The sketches which Whymper brought back from his first Alpine journey delighted William Longman, who commissioned further work. Next year Whymper returned to the Alps. It was on this, his second Alpine tour, that he graduated as a mountaineer. In 1860 he had varied mountain walks with some mild scrambling, but his first real peak was Mont Pelvoux (12,947 feet) in the Dauphiné, which he climbed on August 5, 1861 with R. J. S. Macdonald and Jean Reynaud and local guides (the first British ascent).

After leaving the Dauphiné, Whymper spent some days examining the Mont Cenis tunnel, and then made his way to Breuil in the Valtournanche, the starting point of the ascent of the Matterhorn from Italy.

'Two summits,' writes Whymper, 'amongst those in the Alps which yet remained virgin had excited my admiration. One of these had been attacked numerous times by good mountaineers without success; the other, surrounded by traditional inaccessibility, was almost untouched. These mountains were the Weisshorn and the Matterhorn.'

At Châtillon, Whymper learned that Professor John Tyndall had climbed the Weisshorn and was already at Breuil hoping 'to crown his first victory by another and still greater one'. At Châtillon Whymper had collected a guide who merely served to confirm the low impression which he had already formed of guides in general. He needed a second and a better guide, and everybody in the Valtournanche agreed that Jean Antoine Carrel was 'the cock of the valley'.

'We sought, of course, for Carrel,' writes Whymper, 'and found him a well-made, resolute-looking fellow, with a certain defiant air, which was rather taking. Yes, he would go. Twenty francs a day, whatever the result, was his price. I assented. But I must take his comrade. "Why so?" Oh, it was impossible to get along without another man. As he said this an evil countenance came forth out of the darkness and proclaimed itself the comrade. I demurred, the negotiations broke off, and we went up to Breuil.'

Few of the actors in the drama of the Matterhorn command greater respect than Jean Antoine Carrel. He was first and foremost a great Italian. He had fought in the Italian War of Liberation, and undoubtedly felt that the battle for the Matterhorn was yet another campaign in which the honour of Italy was involved. Naturally he was ambitious to make the first ascent of the Matterhorn, but above all he wanted to lead an Italian party to the summit by way of the Italian ridge.

There were some well-known guides at Breuil when Whymper reached the village, among them Matthias zum Taugwald and 'a sturdy old fellow—Peter Taugwalder by name' who was later to accompany Whymper on the first ascent of the Matterhorn. Not for the last time Whymper found that capable guides either flatly refused to attempt the peak, as did Matthias zum Taugwald, or named a prohibitive price as did Peter Taugwalder— two hundred francs, whether the attempt succeeded or failed.

'This, it may be said once for all, was the reason why so many futile attempts were made upon the Matterhorn. One first-rate guide after another was brought up to the mountain, and patted on the back, but all declined the business. The men who went had no heart in the matter, and took the first opportunity to turn back.'

With the exception of Carrel, all the guides whom Whymper approached were convinced that 'the summit was entirely inaccessible'.

Nothing daunted, Whymper set out to explore the Matterhorn, passed the night in the highest cowshed in the valley, and the next day climbed the south-west ridge and reached the 'chimney'. Whymper's guide not only failed to lead up the chimney but refused to follow after Whymper had got up unassisted. Indeed, he untied himself and announced that he was going down to the valley. Thus ended the first of Whymper's seven attempts on the Italian ridge.

We identify Whymper in our minds with the conquest of the Matterhorn, and it is therefore difficult to remember that the young climber, aged twenty-two, who set out with an incompetent guide to explore the Italian ridge of the Matterhorn, was the veriest novice, his only experience of serious mountaineering being his ascent of the comparatively easy Mont Pelvoux. And yet this novice did not hesitate to attack a peak which many competent guides were unwilling to attempt. Fortunately, Whymper was not only a man of dauntless courage and immense determination but he was also endowed with a natural genius for mountaineering.

On July 18, 1862, Whymper started alone, and next day this solitary climber reached the highest point until then attained on the Matterhorn, nearly 13,500 feet above the sea, a fantastic achievement. On his return he slipped while attempting to turn a corner near the Tête du Lion. He shot down an ice slope, somersaulted, and was thrown from one side of the gully to the other. His fall was finally checked on the verge of a precipice about 200 feet below the point from which he fell. He plastered up the many wounds in his head with snow before scrambling up to a place of safety where he fainted. He managed to make his way down to Breuil, and within a week was making his fifth attempt on the Matterhorn.

His description of what he felt during the fall is particularly convincing to those who, like the present writer, have survived similar experiences.

'I was perfectly conscious of what was happening, and felt each blow; but, like a patient under chloroform, experienced no pain. Each blow was, naturally, more severe than that which preceded it, and I distinctly remember thinking, "Well, if the next is harder still, that will be the end!" Like persons who have been rescued from drowning, I remember that the recollection of a multitude of things rushed through my head, many of them trivialities or absurdities, which had been forgotten long before; and, more remarkable, this bounding through space did not feel disagreeable.'

Four days after Whymper's sensational escape he was again attacking the Matterhorn with Jean Antoine and Caesar Carrel and the porter Luc Meynet, an attempt which was ruined by the weather. Carrel professed himself ready to start again, but on the morning of July 25th Whymper's porter, Luc Meynet, told him that the Carrels had left word that they were spending the day marmot-hunting. Nothing daunted, Whymper decided to see how far up the Matterhorn he could get with Luc Meynet who had already, writes Whymper,

'proved invaluable as a tent-bearer; for—though his legs were more picturesque than symmetrical, and although he seemed to be built on principle with no two parts alike—his very deformities proved of service; and we quickly found he had spirit of no common order, and that few peasants are more agreeable companions, or better climbers, than little Luc Meynet, the hunchback of Breuil. He now showed himself not less serviceable as a scavenger, and humbly asked for gristly pieces of meat, rejected by the others, or for suspicious eggs; and seemed to consider it a peculiar favour, if not a treat, to be permitted to drink the coffee-grounds. With the greatest contentment he took the worst place at the door of the tent, and did all the dirty work which was put upon him by the guides as gratefully as a dog—who has been well beaten—will receive a stroke.'

Luc Meynet was one of those exceptional *Berglers* who had a genuine love of mountain scenery. When they stood together on the Col du Lion it was the first time that Luc Meynet had seen the view unclouded. 'The poor little deformed peasant gazed upon it silently and reverently for a time, and then, unconsciously, fell on one knee in an attitude of adoration, and clasped his hands, exclaiming in ecstasy, "Oh, beautiful mountains!" His actions were as appropriate as his words were natural, and tears bore witness to the reality of his emotion.'

Whymper and his hunchback porter reached a height of 13,160 feet above the sea. Once again Whymper without guides had reached a higher point on the Matterhorn than any guide or amateur had previously reached.

On his return to Breuil, he learned that Professor John Tyndall had arrived during his absence with his two Swiss guides, Johann

Joseph Bennen, who was killed two years later by an avalanche while attempting a winter ascent of the Haut de Cry, and Anton Walter. Tyndall engaged the Carrels as porters.

Whymper generously placed his tent at Tyndall's disposal. Tyndall, according to his account in the second edition of *Hours of Exercise in the Alps*, obtained Bennen's grudging admission that Whymper should be included 'provided that he proved reasonable'. Whymper's reply to an invitation was, 'If I go up the Matterhorn I must lead the way'. Tyndall adds that he thought this reply the reverse of reasonable, and the invitation was accordingly withdrawn. Whymper in a letter to the *Alpine Journal* categorically denied Tyndall's account of their discussion, and stated that Tyndall, after accepting Whymper's offer of his tent, said,'in a way which I thought seemed to imply that the answer might not be in the affirmative, "Mr Whymper, would you like to accompany us?"' And when Whymper accepted with the greatest pleasure, Tyndall added, 'If you go with us, you must place yourself under Bennen's guidance; you must obey his instructions; you must follow his lead'.

Whymper was, of course, ready to accept Bennen's leadership, but 'being called upon to declare that I would implicitly obey his instructions, whether they were right or wrong, I could hardly avoid saying, "You will remember, Dr Tyndall, that I have been much higher than Bennen, and have been eleven days on the mountain, whilst he has been on it only for a single day; you will not expect me to follow him if he is evidently wrong?"' Half an hour later Tyndall came to him and said, 'Well, after all, I think you had better not accompany us'.

Next day Tyndall's party were seen beyond a point which Whymper believed was the key to the ascent. If the point could be passed success was certain. 'I could not bring myself to leave until the result was heard, and lingered about as a foolish lover hovers round the object of his affections, even after he has been contemptuously rejected. The sun had set before the men were descried coming over the pastures. There was no spring in their steps—they, too, were defeated. The Carrels hid their heads, and the others said, as men will do when they have been beaten, that the mountain was horrible, impossible, and so forth. Professor Tyndall told me they had arrived *within a stone's-throw of the summit.*'

In an article published in the *Saturday Review* (August 3, 1863) Tyndall stated that he had reached a point 200 feet below the summit. Actually he was neither within a stone's-throw nor within 200 vertical feet of the summit, for the point he reached was no less than 800 feet lower than the highest point, an interesting example of the power of personal vanity to corrupt the habits of exact observation which Tyndall, as a distinguished scientist, must inevitably have acquired.

Tyndall in his account attributed the failure to the Carrels. Bennen, he implied, would have been ready to continue. The Carrels, according to what they told Whymper when appealed to for their opinion, gave as their answer, 'We are porters, ask your guide'. The cause of Tyndall's defeat was, as Whymper insisted, that the Carrels would not act as guides after having been hired as porters.

John Tyndall was one of the outstanding mountaineers of the Golden Age. He made the first ascent of the Weisshorn and a solitary ascent of Monte Rosa, a remarkable achievement. He was the son of an Irish shoemaker, but such was the prestige of science in the class-conscious Victorian age that the Duke of Abercorn's sister was delighted when he married her daughter. Tyndall was never rich and often poor, but such was his fantastic disinterestedness in money matters that he offered to settle five hundred a year on a friend who fell ill, and when this was declined gave him a hundred pounds. He invested the net profit of his first lecture tour in America, £2,500, to found Tyndall scholarships, but though generous in money matters he was ungenerous in controversy.

His controversy with Whymper after Tyndall's defeat on the Matterhorn was full of mis-statements, and an insinuation in a later reference to the Matterhorn accident is indefensible in the view of Lord Schuster, sometime President of the Alpine Club. Tyndall not only quarrelled with fellow mountaineers but also with fellow scientists. His bitter and wholly unjustified attack on J. D. Forbes, the eminent glaciologist and first honorary member of the Alpine Club, shocked the leaders of the Alpine Club, notably the gentle and judicial Alfred Wills. Forbes' reply was completely convincing, but Tyndall refused either to withdraw his charges or to prove them. Like many aggressive controver-

6. (a) Jean-Antoine Carrel
   (b) *Michel-Auguste Croz*

[reproduced from Whymper's
Scrambles Amongst the Alps]

(a)

7. (a) Lord Francis Douglas
   (b) The Rev. Charles Hudson

(b)

[reproduced from Whymper's
Scrambles Amongst the Alps]

sialists he took refuge, when cornered, in a smug protest against controversy as such. 'I have abstained from answering my distinguished censor, not from inability to do so, but because I thought and think that, within the limits of the case, it is better to submit to misconception than to make science the field of personal controversy.' Tyndall was persuaded to withdraw a resignation which he threatened when his attack on Forbes lost him the presidency of the Alpine Club, but two years later he resigned as a protest against some jesting remarks by Leslie Stephen at the winter dinner of the Alpine Club, remarks which, in his opinion, 'reflected upon the value of science in connection with mountaineering'. The substance of these jests was later reproduced in Stephen's *The Playground of Europe.*

' "And what philosophical observations did you make?" will be the enquiry of one of those fanatics who, by a reasoning process to me utterly inscrutable, have somehow irrevocably associated alpine travelling with science. To them I answer that the temperature on the summit of the Zinal Rothorn was approximately (I had no thermometer) 212 (Fahrenheit) below freezing point. As for ozone, if any existed in the atmosphere, it was a greater fool than I take it for.'

D

CHAPTER VIII

Penultimate

Whymper made his seventh attempt on the Matterhorn a fortnight after Tyndall's failure, and once again by the same Italian ridge up which all the earliest attempts on the Matterhorn had been made by the Carrels in the years 1858 and 1859. That the Carrels should concentrate on the Italian ridge was understandable, but that Whymper should apparently never have contemplated an attack from Zermatt until 1865 is all the more difficult to understand in view of the fact that in 1860 and 1861 attempts had been made by the Zermatt route. In July 1860 the three brothers Alfred, Charles and Sandbach Parker of Liverpool, without guides, reached a height of 12,000 feet on the east face before they were turned back by storm. In July 1861 the three brothers made a second attempt by the same route, and reached a point rather higher than that previously attained before they were defeated by lack of time. They reported that the east face was practicable for many hundred feet above the point from which they retired, but neither Whymper nor any other climber was sufficiently impressed to continue the exploration of what is now known to be the easiest route up the Matterhorn.

I wish we knew more about the Parker brothers, pioneers of guideless climbing, whose finest expedition was the first guideless ascent of the Finsteraarhorn.

Almost as puzzling as the neglect of the east face is the complete absence of all attempts on the Matterhorn in 1864. Why did Whymper, whose supreme ambition was to make the first ascent, devote all his energies to the Dauphiné, where he made the first ascent of the Ecrins, and to the Mont Blanc range, where his party made the first ascent of the Aiguille d'Argentière and the Mont Dolent?

Finally, on June 14, 1865, Whymper made his penultimate attempt on the Matterhorn by the most absurd of routes. By this time he had begun to suspect that the east face would prove the easiest route to the summit, but his guide, Michel Croz, still believed the mountain to be inaccessible on the Zermatt side, and Whymper decided to investigate one more possibility before attempting the east face. The 'possibility' in question was to ascend by a gully to a point on the Furggen ridge from which he could traverse the east face to the shoulder on the north-east ridge. The entire route to the shoulder was liable to be swept by falling stones, and in fact the grotesque attempt was abandoned after a narrow escape from falling stones in the gully.

What Whymper had seen of the east face convinced him that Croz was mistaken, and after the retreat from the gully Whymper decided to cross the Furggjoch, bivouac on the Hörnli, and attempt the Matterhorn next day by the eastern route. Had this plan been carried out, it is probable that Whymper would have succeeded. Bad weather and the opposition of his guides— 'Why don't you try,' asked Almer, 'to go up a mountain which can be ascended?'—compelled a retreat to Breuil.

Next day Whymper left for the Mont Blanc range where he made the first ascents of the Aiguille Verte, the western summit of the Grandes Jorasses, which is not the highest point, and the first traverse of the Col du Dolent and the Col de Talèfre. On his high-level return route to Zermatt he made the first ascent of the Ruinette.

His guides, Christian Almer and Franz Biener, were dismayed by Whymper's decision to attempt the Matterhorn. '*Anything but the Matterhorn, dear sir!*' said Almer. '*Anything but the Matterhorn.*' 'For their own credit,' writes Whymper, 'as well as for my sake, they did not wish to undertake a business which, in their opinion, would only lead to loss of time and money.'

Whymper walked down the Valtournanche to look for Jean Antoine Carrel, only to learn that he had started the previous day for the Matterhorn on which Whymper knew they could not succeed because the weather was unsatisfactory. In fact he met them on their return, and Carrel agreed to cross the Théodule and attempt the Matterhorn from Zermatt. 'I then went up to Breuil,' writes Whymper, 'and discharged Almer and

Biener—with much regret, for no two men ever served me more faithfully or more willingly.'

The 8th was occupied with preparations. On the 9th a young man came up from the Valtournanche to report that an Englishman was lying there extremely ill. Now Whymper, when he was recovering from his fall on the Col du Lion, had vowed that 'if an Englishman should at any time fall sick in the Val Tournanche, he should not feel so solitary as I did at this dreary time', so when he heard of the sick Englishman he felt that the time had come 'for the performance of my vow', and on the 9th went down the valley to look after the sick man. He was in need of medicine, so Whymper tramped down to Châtillon to get it. On the sick man declaring that he was better, Whymper made ready to start again, only to discover that Carrel now declared that he was committed by a previous engagement to 'travel with a party of ladies'. 'That work is not fit for you', said Whymper. Carrel smiled grimly, for he knew that the task which had been assigned to him was more fitted for him than for any other man. It was only after Carrel had left for the Matterhorn that Whymper discovered that he had been 'bamboozled and humbugged'.

What had happened was this. In 1863 some leading Italian mountaineers, among them two distinguished scientists, Felice Giordano and Quintino Sella, founded the Italian Alpine Club in Turin. They resolved that as English climbers had robbed them of Monte Viso, prince of Piedmontese peaks, Italians should have the honour of making the first ascent of the Matterhorn.

On July 7, 1865, Giordano had written to Sella, 'Let us, then, set out to attack this Devil's mountain; and let us see that we succeed, if only Whymper has not been beforehand'. On the 11th he wrote again:

"We immediately sent off our advance guard with Carrel at its head. In order not to excite remark, we took the rope and other materials to Avouil, a hamlet which is very remote and close to the Matterhorn; and this is to be our lower base. . . . I have tried to keep everything secret; but that fellow whose life seems to depend on the Matterhorn, is here suspiciously prying into everything. I have taken all the best men away from him;

and yet he is so enamoured of the mountain that he may go with others and make a scene. He is here in the hotel and I try to avoid speaking to him.'

Whymper decided to cross the Théodule to Zermatt and engage the first competent guide that he could find for an attack on the mountain from Switzerland. At this point Lord Francis Douglas, who had just made the second ascent of the Gabelhorn, and the first from Zinal, arrived from Zermatt. He confided to Whymper that Peter Taugwalder had prospected the east face of the Matterhorn and was confident that it could be climbed. Graham Brown, writing in the *Alpine Journal*, gives his reasons for supposing that Douglas had come to Breuil to engage Carrel and that Whymper gate-crashed into his expedition. 'There is therefore', he writes, 'something magnificent in Whymper's words about Douglas: "Before long it was determined that he should take part in the expedition".'

On the 12th they crossed to Zermatt and engaged old Peter Taugwalder. On his return to the Monte Rosa Hotel, Whymper was delighted to see his old guide, Michel Croz, sitting on the wall in front of the hotel. Croz had left Whymper as the result of a misunderstanding, but his employer had fallen ill. Croz had immediately been engaged by the Rev. Charles Hudson, and they had just arrived in Zermatt 'with the same objective as ourselves—namely to attempt the ascent of the Matterhorn'.

Hudson, who, according to Leslie Stephen, was 'as simple and noble a character as ever carried out the precepts of muscular Christianity without talking its cant', was the greatest amateur of the day, a pioneer of guideless climbing who had led a guideless party up Mont Blanc by a new route. He did not waste time attempting the more difficult Italian routes but determined to attack the Matterhorn from Zermatt. Hudson's friend, Douglas Hadow, a young man of nineteen who had just left Harrow, was included in the party. According to Hudson, he 'had done Mont Blanc in less time than most men', but though a strong walker he was an inexperienced climber. Whymper and Hudson agreed that it was 'undesirable that two independent parties should be on the mountain at the same time and with the same object', and it was therefore decided to join forces.

'So Croz and I became comrades once more; and as I threw myself on my bed and tried to go to sleep, I wondered at the strange series of chances which had first separated us and then brought us together again. I thought of the mistake through which he had accepted the engagement to Mr B.; of his unwillingness to adopt my route; of his recommendation to transfer our energies to the chain of Mont Blanc; of the retirement of Almer and Biener; of the desertion of Carrel; of the arrival of Lord Francis Douglas; and, lastly, of our accidental meeting at Zermatt; and as I pondered over these things I could not help asking, "What next?" '

Of all the guides with whom Whymper climbed, Michel Croz, he tells us,

'was the man who was most after my own heart. He did not work like a blunt razor, and take to his toil unkindly. He did not need urging, or to be told a second time to do anything. You had only to say *what* was to be done, and *how* it was to be done, and the work *was* done, if it was possible. Such men are not common, and when they are known they are valued. Michel was not widely known, but those who did know him came again and again. The inscription that is placed upon his tomb truthfully records that he was "beloved by his comrades and esteemed by travellers".'

NOTE

Douglas Hadow, the son of Patrick Hadow, was the eldest of a family of eight boys and one girl. All the sons went to Harrow excepting Reginald, who went into the Navy. Another brother, Patrick, was the second Wimbledon Tennis Singles Champion, in 1878. At the time of the accident Charles Hudson was tutoring Douglas Hadow, having previously tutored Lord Francis Douglas. The Queensberry and Hadow families were close friends and neighbours.

CHAPTER IX

Triumph and Tragedy

Whymper, Charles Hudson, Lord Francis Douglas, Douglas Hadow, Michel Croz, Peter Taugwalder, and his two sons who were engaged as porters, left Zermatt at half-past five on the morning of July 13, 1865. At 11.30 a.m. they had started up the actual peak, and 'were astonished to find that places which from the Riffel, or even from the Furggengletscher, looked entirely impracticable, were so easy that we could *run about*'.

They camped at 11,000 feet. Croz and young Peter went on to explore the route, and returned three hours later with the good news that there was 'not a single difficulty! We could have gone to the summit and returned to-day easily!'

'Long after dusk,' writes Whymper, 'the cliffs above echoed with our laughter and with the songs of the guides, for we were happy that night in camp, and feared no evil.'

They left next morning as soon as it was light enough to move. The youngest Taugwalder returned to Zermatt. The climbing presented no real difficulties. 'When an obstruction was met in front it could always be turned to the right or to the left. For the greater part of the way there was, indeed, no occasion for the rope, and sometimes Hudson led, sometimes myself.' At a height of 14,000 feet, which they reached at 9.55, they rested for fifty minutes and then climbed the snow shoulder. From the top of this shoulder the modern route leads direct to the summit, keeping very near the Hörnli ridge, for fixed ropes facilitate the ascent of the steepest pitches, but in 1865 Whymper's party were forced on to the north face.

' "Now," said Croz, as he led off, "now for something altogether different." The work became difficult and required caution. In some places there was little to hold, and it was desirable that those should be in front who were least likely to slip. The general slope of the mountain at this part was *less* than forty degrees, and snow had accumulated in, and had filled up, the interstices of the rock face, leaving only occasional fragments projecting here and there. These were at times covered with a thin film of ice, produced from the melting and refreezing of the snow.'

Hadow 'was not accustomed to this kind of work, and required continual assistance. It is only fair to say that the difficulty which he found at this part arose simply and entirely from want of experience.' Whymper estimates that they spent about an hour and a half on this difficult section. 'A long stride round a rather awkward corner brought us to snow once more. The last doubt vanished! The Matterhorn was ours! Nothing but 200 feet of easy snow remained to be surmounted!'

But it was not yet certain that the Italians who had started from Breuil on the 11th had not beaten them.

'All the way up we had talked of them, and many false alarms of "men on the summit" had been raised. The higher we rose, the more intense became the excitement. What if we should be beaten at the last moment? The slope eased off, at length we could be detached, and Croz and I, dashing away, ran a neck-and-neck race, which ended in a dead heat. At 1.40 p.m. the world was at our feet, and the Matterhorn was conquered. Hurrah! Not a footstep could be seen.

'It was not yet certain that we had not been beaten. The summit of the Matterhorn was formed of a rudely level ridge, about 350 feet long, and the Italians might have been at its farther extremity. I hastened to the southern end, scanning the snow right and left eagerly. Hurrah! again; it was untrodden — "Where were the men?" I peered over the cliff, half doubting, half expectant, and saw them immediately—mere dots on the ridge, at an immense distance below.'

They shouted until they were hoarse, and then hurled stones down the cliff, near enough to the Italians to arouse their attention. Croz took one of the poles of the tent which they had brought with them, and, pulling off his blouse, fixed it to the stick.

'They saw it at Zermatt—at the Riffel—in the Val Tournanche. At Breuil the watchers cried, "Victory is ours!" They raised "bravos" for Carrel and "vivas" for Italy, and hastened to put themselves *en fête*. On the morrow they were undeceived. "All was changed; the explorers returned sad—cast down—disheartened—confounded—gloomy." "It is true", said the men. "We saw them ourselves—they hurled stones at us! The old traditions *are* true—there are spirits on the top of the Matterhorn!"'

Nonsense. We know what Carrel reported to Giordano on his return. He did not mistake Whymper for a demon. He recognised him by his white trousers. This was yet another example of Whymper's habit of picturesque invention.

They remained on the summit for an hour, revelling in their triumph. They seem to have been too intoxicated by victory to devote sufficient thought to the problem of security on the descent. Whymper stayed behind to write their names in a bottle to be left on the summit. 'A few minutes afterwards I tied myself to young Peter, ran down after the others, and caught them just as they were commencing the descent of the difficult part.' Whymper and young Taugwalder then tied themselves on to the rest of the party.

Could there be a more casual preparation for a dangerous descent? The first blunder was that young Peter Taugwalder was the last man down. The most experienced mountaineer should have the post of honour on the descent, bringing up the rear. The second blunder was to ignore Whymper's sound proposal that some of their ample spare rope should be attached to the rocks as additional security for the descent of the difficult part. The worst blunder was to use the weakest rope to link old Taugwalder and Lord Francis Douglas.

And this is what happened.

Michel Croz had laid aside his axe to take hold of Hadow's legs to place his feet in secure positions. Both men were hidden from Whymper when Hadow slipped.

'I heard one startled exclamation from Croz, then saw him

and Mr. Hadow flying downwards; in another moment Hudson
was dragged from his steps, and Lord F. Douglas immediately
after him. All this was the work of a moment. Immediately we
heard Croz's exclamation, old Peter and I planted ourselves as
firmly as the rocks would permit: the rope was taut between
us, and the jerk came on us both as on one man. We held; but
the rope broke midway between Taugwalder and Lord Francis
Douglas. For a few seconds we saw our unfortunate companions sliding downwards on their backs, and spreading out
their hands, endeavouring to save themselves. They passed from
our sight uninjured, disappeared one by one, and fell from
precipice to precipice on to the Matterhorngletscher below, a
distance of nearly 4,000 feet in height. From the moment the
rope broke it was impossible to help them.

'So perished our comrades! For the space of half an hour we
remained on the spot without moving a single step.'

The two men were 'paralyzed by terror'. When they had re-
covered, Whymper asked for the rope which had broken, and
found to his horror that it was the weakest of the three ropes.

'It was intended as a reserve, in case we had to leave much
rope behind, attached to rocks. I saw at once that a serious
question was involved, and made him give me the end. It had
broken in mid-air, and it did not appear to have sustained
previous injury.'

At 6 p.m. they reached the snow shoulder and all danger
was over. Suddenly a mighty arch appeared in the sky 'rising
above the Lyskamm' which gradually developed into two vast
crosses. Is there any independent evidence for a phenomenon
which must have been visible behind the Lyskamm from the
Gornergrat, which was much frequented in fine weather, and
from many other viewpoints above Zermatt?

They passed six miserable hours of darkness on the mountain,
and resumed the descent at daybreak.

'Seiler', writes Whymper, 'met me at his door, and followed
in silence to my room. "What is the matter?" "The Taugwalders
and I have returned." He did not need more, and burst into
tears; but lost no time in useless lamentations, and set to work

to arouse the village. Ere long a score of men had started to ascend the Hohlicht heights, above Kalbermatt and Z'Mutt, which commanded the plateau of the Matterhorngletscher. They returned after six hours, and reported that they had seen the bodies lying motionless on the snow.'

Just before leaving for the Matterhorn, Hudson had written a letter to an old friend, the Rev. Joseph McCormick: 'We and Whymper are just off to try the Cervin. You can hear about our movements from the landlord of the Monte Rosa Hotel.' On the morning of Whymper's return to Zermatt, McCormick had left for the Gornergrat. On his return he found a letter from Whymper asking him if he would join the search party, 'as I particularly wish to have an Englishman with me.'

The search party started at 2 a.m. on Sunday the 16th.

'By 8.30,' writes Whymper, 'we had got to the plateau at the top of the glacier, and within sight of the corner in which we knew my companions must be. As we saw one weather-beaten man after another raise the telescope, turn deadly pale, and pass it on without a word to the next, we knew that all hope was gone. We approached. They had fallen below as they had fallen above—Croz a little in advance, Hadow near him, and Hudson some distance behind; but of Lord Francis Douglas we could see nothing. We left them where they fell; buried in snow at the base of the grandest cliff of the most majestic mountain of the Alps.'

'A consultation was held,' wrote McCormick, 'as to what had better be done with the bodies, and all were agreed that, taking everything into consideration, the best thing we could do would be to bury them in the snow . . . With our axes we made a grave, cut larger pieces of ice, collected the snow, and covered them over.

'It was suggested that we should have a short funeral service. Poor Hudson's prayer-book was produced for this purpose, but as it was an abridged copy we could not go through the ordinary service of the Church of England. I, therefore, read out of it Psalm XC, so singularly appropriate to time and place, and repeated some prayers and a portion of the burial service. Imagine us standing, with our bronze-faced guides, leaning on our axes or alpenstocks around that newly-made and singular grave, in the centre of a snow-field, perhaps never before trodden by man, with that awful mountain frowning above us, under a cloudless sky.'[1]

The local authorities, however, decided that the bodies were to be brought down to the valley.

'The remains of Hudson and Hadow were interred upon the north side of the Zermatt church, in the presence of a reverent crowd of sympathizing friends. The body of Michel Croz lies upon the other side, under a simpler tomb, whose inscription bears honourable testimony to his rectitude, to his courage, and to his devotion.'

Hudson's body was later transferred to the Anglican church and buried beneath the high altar, as is recorded on a tablet which reads as follows:

> Beneath the Holy Table, waiting for
> the coming of our Lord Jesus Christ
> now lie the earthly remains of
> Charles Hudson, Vicar of Skillington
> Lincolnshire (killed on the Matterhorn
> July 14, 1865) removed hither after
> resting for forty-six years in the Village Church.

The Anglican church in Zermatt is known as 'the Parish Church of the Alpine Club', and contains many tablets which include memorials to Clinton Dent who made the first ascent of the Dru, Edward Alfred Broome and Owen Glynne Jones, killed on the Dent Blanche.

The body of Lord Francis Douglas has never been found. *Coelo tegitur qui non urnam habet.*

NOTE

Many years after the accident, Canon McCormick told the story of the search party to a boy of ten who had read and re-read Whymper's *Scrambles*. McCormick seems to have assumed that the boy in question was not only interested in mountains but also in cricket, for twenty-five years later I was astonished to be informed by the Secretary of the M.C.C. that I had been elected a member of that august society on the proposal of the late Canon J. McCormick.

[1] From a pamphlet *A Sad Holiday*. A lecture delivered before Liverpool College, by the Rev. Joseph McCormick.

CHAPTER X

Aftermath

In 1865 mountaineering was still regarded as the sport of a few eccentrics, and few Zermatters were particularly interested in the party which left the village on July 13 to attempt the Matterhorn. Herr Karl Lehner, who has made a study of local traditions, tells me that an old lady who was a girl at the time heard somebody say that men had been seen on the top of the Matterhorn, and remembered that those to whom this information had been imparted showed no interest. Alexander Seiler, of course, was interested, but when he rushed into the dining room to announce that there were men on the Matterhorn, half the guests refused to leave the table and continued placidly eating.

It was the tragedy rather than the triumph which attracted world-wide attention. Indeed, no accident in the history of mountaineering has ever created such a sensation. Scandalmongers were busy from the first. Rumours were spread that the rope had been cut. If one of two climbers falls into a concealed crevasse, his companion might find it impossible to pull him out, and in this case he might be tempted to cut the rope, but on a rock face on which there are, as there were on the Matterhorn, abundant foot- and hand-holds, there is nothing to be gained by cutting the rope once a fall has been checked, and obviously there is no time to extract a knife and cut the rope in mid-air before the fall is checked.

When Hadow slipped[1] there were three possibilities: (1) that the rope would not break and that Taugwalder would suc-

---

[1] It is, as Frank Smythe rightly remarked, 'an assumption that Hadow slipped in the first place. It was impossible for Whymper to suppose that Croz could slip, yet Emile Rey, the greatest guide of his generation, slipped on easy ground and was killed.' Op. cit. p. 204.

ceed in checking the fall without being dragged off the rocks; in that case nobody would have been killed; (2) that the entire party would be dragged off the rocks; (3) that the weak rope would break leaving the Taugwalders and Whymper on the face of the mountain. Responsible critics did not suggest foul play. It was mountaineers in general rather than the Matterhorn mountaineers in particular who were the target for criticisms.

A leading article in *The Times* (July 27, 1865) probably expressed what most of its readers felt about mountaineering. As Smythe remarks, 'It was legitimate for men to break their necks steeplechasing or on the hunting field, but not on a mountain.'

'There are occasions,' wrote *The Times*, 'on which a journal must brave certain unpopularity and ridicule, even in quarters where it may most wish to stand well. We desire the sympathies of the young, the courageous, and the enterprising, and we can feel their taunts. But we have our Matterhorn to ascend as well as they—not without cause. Why is the best blood of England to waste itself in scaling hitherto inaccessible peaks, in staining the eternal snow, and reaching the unfathomable abyss never to return? . . . Life requires a great deal of courage, moral as well as physical, whatever the meaning of the distinction. Every gentleman with a sphere of duties and a station in society requires courage and presence of mind, otherwise he is sure to be scorned and to become an object of civil contempt. A man cannot hold his own in a parish vestry, or on the committee of a coal fund, without knowing what he is about, and standing to his colours and defending his rights. If he has not this courage, he had better purchase a lathe, or write metaphysics, for he is good for nothing out of doors. But this courage is not acquired in a succession of desperate adventures. The Age of Chivalry is over . . . But, of course, our young men will go to Switzerland, and they will ascend mountains, and they will feel a very natural and irresistible desire to do what everybody has done before them, and, still more, what nobody has done. This is the great prize which caps and leads on the lesser attempts. It was the blue riband of the Alps that poor Lord Francis Douglas was trying for the other day. If it must be so, at all events the Alpine Club, that has proclaimed this crusade, must manage the thing rather better, or it will soon be voted a nuisance. If the work is to be done, it must be done well.'

Other periodicals were even more critical, and the *Standard* was positively scurilous.

Queen Victoria was deeply shocked, and asked the Lord Chamberlain if something could not be done to stop mountaineering by law. At Zermatt Whymper had decided to write nothing about the accident but could not resist a moving appeal from Alfred Wills, the President of the Alpine Club, who wrote a letter eventually published in *The Times* of August 8th.

'Dear Whymper,

'I cannot refrain from asking you to accept the assurance of my deep and heartfelt sympathy with you in the terrible and afflicting circumstances in which you have so lately been placed; and I advisedly name yourself first, for there are few men who would not feel that in many respects it were more tolerable to be of the lost than of the survivors. If the sympathy and confidence of your friends can be of any avail, I think I may assure you you will have it freely; for I think it will not be suspected by anyone who knows you that with two such mountaineers as yourself and Hudson of the party any reasonable precaution was likely to be neglected, so far as you and he, at all events, were concerned. I speak only of you and him, because I did not know the others. Hudson I did know, and therefore know that there never was a man who had a more active frame, a more steady hand, or head, or foot, a firmer mind in danger, or a more keen and scrupulous sense of right and wrong. A man more unlikely rashly or inconsiderately to put in jeopardy his own life and that of others I never knew, and this not because he feared danger when it came in a proper way, but because he appreciated too highly the ties that bound him for the sake of himself and others to life and duty.

'But may I make an appeal to you to relieve those who take an interest in this sad matter from the state of anxiety and suspense in which your own silence—a silence which I understand and respect—has kept us . . .

'Believe me, dear Whymper,
'Yours most truly,
(*Signed*) ALFRED WILLS

Whymper's reply, written at Haslemere and dated August 7, was published in *The Times* of August 8, but Whymper's letter to *The Times* was not, as Smythe implies, Whymper's first written statement about the accident. His first communication was sent not to the Secretary of the Alpine Club, but in a letter dated July 26 and written at Interlaken, to the Secretary of the Italian Alpine Club. This was published in the *Bollettino del* C.A.L. 1865, n.I. pp 20-25, and reprinted in Alfonso Bernardi's excellent anthology, *Il Gran Cervino*.

In this, as in the letter to *The Times*, he writes with great bitterness of the Taugwalders, perhaps because Alfred Wills had been too generous in assuming that he had neglected no 'reasonable precaution'. (See page 63.) Self-reproach is only too easily transmuted into bitter reproaches of other people. His original attacks on the Taugwalders were amplified in *Scrambles amongst the Alps*. He did his best to create an impression of impartiality by defending the older Taugwalder from the charge, which no responsible person ever made, that he cut the rope, and substituted three accusations of his own.

(1) Whymper implies that Taugwalder deliberately tied himself to Douglas with a weak rope as a protection in case of an accident. We have seen (page 56) that Croz and Whymper were so excited when they approached the summit that they detached themselves from the rope. 'Detached' is Whymper's word. Actually the rope was cut. In 1949 a friend of mine in the Alpine Club, the late Geoffrey Howard, repeated a story on A. E. W. Mason's authority, a story which he confirmed in a letter. Whymper, after a good dinner, remarked to Mason, 'Thinking it over, I believe that I did cut the rope behind me so that I could more easily race Croz to the top.' If this was so, bad rope may have been used because the better rope was cut by Whymper and, in fairness to a great guide, this relevant evidence should not have been suppressed.

(2) Whymper stated that the Taugwalders asked him to make a statement in their *Führerbuch* to the effect that they had not been paid. Whymper assumed that their intention was thereby to arouse sympathy and perhaps increase their clientele. Whymper knew no German, and the only means of communication between him and the Taugwalders was French. Now in an

The first ascent of the Matterhorn, from an engraving by Gustave Doré

9. The tragedy on the Matterhorn, from an engraving by Gustave Doré

article which I contributed to *The Alpine Journal* (Vol. LV., p. 290, May 1946) I have shown that Whymper's knowledge of French was almost non-existent and that Taugwalder had probably only acquired a rudimentary knowledge of the French patois spoken in the Valtournanche to which he had once paid a long visit. My own guess is that the Taugwalders *did* make some reference to the *Führerbuch*, in which mountaineers are expected to record their appreciation of the services rendered by their guides, and that what they wanted was some statement clearing them of responsibility for the accident. Nobody with any real knowledge of the outlook of a mountain peasant would credit the Taugwalders with offering to forego immediate payment for services rendered in the far-fetched hope of recouping themselves later, thanks to the sympathy thus aroused.

(3) In a memorandum of a communication made to John Jermyn Cowell, Honorary Secretary of the Alpine Club, by Whymper, it was stated that Whymper passed a miserable night, and that the demeanour of the Taugwalders

'gradually became and continued to be suggestive of personal danger to himself—that at night they, as it were, hustled him to induce him to attempt the further descent by moonlight—that thereafter they urged him to lie down in a manner so importunate and minatory as to induce him to place himself with his back to a rock and with his axe in his hand to order them to keep at a greater distance from him—and that he passed the night standing in that manner and prepared to defend himself. The inferences which arose in our minds were that the Taugwalders saw that the additional loss of Whymper would afford them an opening to a future notoriety of a very lucrative nature, and that they were prepared to avail themselves of any opportunity that might offer during the descent of bringing about that loss.'

Whymper relegated to a footnote the one tribute which he paid to Taugwalder. 'Not only was his act at the critical moment wonderful as a feat of strength, but it was admirable in its performance at the right time.'

Whymper was the hero of Smythe's youth, and this perhaps explains his strange remark that 'it was Whymper's concern

E

before anything else to clear the old man's character, a concern which speaks well for his generosity of spirit.' As Whymper accused Taugwalder not only of protecting himself by deliberately choosing a weak rope between himself and Douglas, but also of plotting his murder, it is interesting to speculate on what charges Whymper might have brought had he been less concerned 'to clear the old man's character', and less generous in spirit.

Smythe emphatically rejects the suggestion that the Taugwalders entertained sinister designs, and attributes Whymper's suspicions to his 'nerve shattering experience' and to a 'hiatus in understanding between them and him.'

There was at least one prominent member of the Alpine Club who defended Taugwalder against Whymper's reckless charges. Leslie Stephen, in a review of Whymper's book which appeared in *Macmillan's* (August 1871) and which was completely forgotten until I discovered and republished it, wrote as follows:

'Knowing the carelessness too often displayed on such occasions, the confidence which guides will show in weak ropes, and the probable state of excitement of the whole party, which would easily account for such an oversight, I think that the hypothesis of deliberate intention on Taugwalder's part is in the highest degree improbable; and there is not a particle of direct evidence in its favour. The presumption would be that Croz was almost equally responsible; and, at any rate, such accusations should have some more tangible ground than a vague possibility.'

At the time, no Swiss amateur, so far as I can discover, defended the Taugwalders, and it is a pity that Herr C. Egger's article which was published in *Die Alpen*, the monthly publication of the Swiss Alpine Club, in July, 1940, was not published seventy years before. Herr Egger was a Swiss pioneer of ski-mountaineering and the author of many scholarly articles on the history of mountaineering.

He was impressed by the clear and logical answers which old Taugwalder gave at the inquiry ('*sont même d'une clarté et d'une logique remarkable*'). Herr Egger is left with the impression that Whymper, consciously or unconsciously, wished to deflect attention from himself to his guides, in order to diminish his own responsibilities for the accident. For Whymper tied himself on to Taugwalder after the delay caused by depositing the names on the summit; he ought therefore to have perceived that it was the weakest rope which united Taugwalder to Douglas, all the more so as he had himself provided the ropes.

No native of Zermatt, in spite of Whymper's assertion to the contrary, ever believed that Taugwalder had cut the rope. The suggestion that Taugwalder emigrated to America because he was under a cloud in his native valley is yet another example of Whymper's inventive powers where some picturesque detail is needed to round off a story. Taugwalder was persuaded to emigrate by the example of many Zermatters at a time when emigration suddenly seemed attractive, and like many of those who did emigrate, he returned to Zermatt.

Though I have spent more of my long life in Switzerland than in my own country, I have no illusions about the difficulties of penetrating the granite curtain which separates the men of the plains from the men of the mountains. Characteristic of this failure of communication was the fact that no British mountaineer was allowed to suspect the depth of the resentment provoked by Whymper's attack on the Taugwalders. If Coolidge, for instance, had known of the valley's attitude to Whymper, he would have been delighted to tell me, for there was no fact discreditable to Whymper and known to Coolidge which he did not communicate to me in the course of our many long conversations when we were both living in Grindelwald.

It was not until I had published in *The Alpine Journal*[1] an article defending the Taugwalders against Whymper's attack that I discovered how bitterly that attack had been resented. It was only then that Joseph Knubel, who had been told about the article, said, 'Whymper *war nicht beliebt in Tal*' (Whymper was not liked in the valley), and that Otto Furrer went out of his way to thank me. 'You were the first', he said, 'to defend the Taugwalders against an unfair attack.' Not the first, but Leslie Stephen's article never reached the valley.

The men of the valley never raised the question with their various mountaineering patrons, with Sir Martin Conway, later Lord Conway of Allington, for instance, who loved Alpine

[1] Vol. LV, p. 290.

gossip, and who was particularly interested in Whymper, whose complex character he often discussed with me. He knew nothing of Zermatt sentiment on this point.

The monument erected since the second world war to Peter Taugwalder and his son was intended to put on record the unanimity with which the Zermatters dismissed Whymper's attack on the Taugwalders. *Berglers* (mountain people) seldom comment in the presence of foreigners on anything which foreigners may say about *Berglers*. No member of the Alpine Club was ever allowed to suspect how much Whymper's attack was resented. The Taugwalders themselves remained silent under accusations which they knew to be false. It was Dr Albert Julen, a priest and a member of a famous Zermatt family, who initiated the monument to the Taugwalders, a monument which by the word *Berufstreue* ,'Faithful to their professional duties', put on record the rejection by the Zermatters of Whymper's insinuations.

The inscription reads:

Peter Taugwalder, Vater und Sohn
Die Berufstreue Führer, Erste besteiger des Matterhorn 1865

'We did not want any polemic,' said the Abbé Julen to me, 'but we just wished to make it known that we knew that they had done their duty.'

CHAPTER XI

Edward Whymper (II)

Whymper was always Seiler's guest when he stayed at the Monte Rosa, but he was expected to pay for his drinks. On one occasion when Whymper reluctantly paid his drink bill he said, 'What would Zermatt be without me?' to which one of Seiler's daughters replied, 'And what would Whymper be but for the Matterhorn?' This was far more realistic than Alexander Seiler's often quoted remark that the Matterhorn was Whymper's 'grösster Unglucksberg' (unluckiest mountain), for the triumph and tragedy of the first ascent promoted this young man of twenty-five from a climber known only to the small fraternity of mountaineers into a world-wide celebrity, a position which he proceeded to exploit with hard-headed realism by his pen and by lecturing, his main sources of income.

Coolidge was certainly not an unbiased critic so far as Whymper was concerned, but many mountaineers would agree with the substance of some remarks which he made to me in the course of one of our Grindelwald meetings.

'Whymper', he began, 'was not a mountaineering genius. He never attempted the obvious route up the Matterhorn till he tacked himself on to Hudson. Now Hudson was the outstanding mountaineer of the day, and if Hudson hadn't been killed, the conquest of the Matterhorn would have been regarded as Hudson's victory. I hope I shan't shock you, Mr Lunn, if I hint that Whymper was lucky that he was the sole survivor of the amateurs in the successful party. I hope you don't think me naughty to suggest that Hudson's death was the basis of Whymper's fame.'

And the sage of Grindelwald gave a happy cackle, the invariable accompaniment of his more feline remarks.

I am writing these lines after spending an hour earlier in the day on the Théodule pass which I reached by ski-lift. I cannot understand how Whymper, who crossed and recrossed this pass several times, cannot have failed to discover that the east face was one vast bluff, for its true character is obvious from the summit of the Théodule. I also examined very carefully the gully by which Whymper attempted to reach a point on the Furggen ridge from which he could traverse the east face to the shoulder. How Whymper or his guides could have conceived that this particular stone-swept gully was easier than the east face is incredible. Whymper, it is true, had begun to suspect that the east face was practicable, but he had wholly failed to impress his views on Croz on the penultimate attempt on June 14, 1865.

'Nineteen days later,' writes Captain J. P. Farrar, 'Croz arrived at Zermatt with Hudson to attempt, as a matter in the ordinary course of his guide's business, the ascent by this very east face. We can reasonably account for this change by the impress of the study, the experience, and the knowledge of his new employer.'[1]

Whymper was, by popular acclaim, the greatest mountaineer of the age, an uninformed verdict which his great book, *Scrambles amongst the Alps*, helped to confirm, and it would seem that he resented any challenge to his position by more expert opinion. He knew that he had attached himself to Hudson's expedition, and must have known that Hudson was a more experienced mountaineer, and this appears to have rankled, with the result that, as Graham Brown, when editor of *The Alpine Journal*, remarked, 'he allowed his bitterness against Hudson to appear in an unfair attack'.

The impression which emerges from Graham Brown's analysis of Whymper's attitude to Hudson is reinforced by an article in the same issue by Mr T. S. Blakeney.

'The Alpine Club has been presented with Whymper's own copy of Mummery's *My Climbs in the Alps and Caucasus*. Against Freshfield's tribute quoted in the preface, "his untimely death is a grievous loss to the Club", Whymper wrote, "I do not agree". In *The Sphere*, January 30, 1909, Whymper reviewed

[1] *Alpine Journal* xxx ii, p. 27

the book and described it as a "vicious" book. A memorandum pasted inside the volume shows that in the event of his review provoking comment he intended "to try and belittle Mummery by quoting my times across the Col Dolent against his across the Col des Courtes, and my times on the Aig. Verte against his times". He then speculates on the conditions in which Mummery's body is likely to be should traces of it be found. "It will be", he says, "in the shape of a dislocated skeleton, one bone here and another there. The stomach and heart will be nowhere". Mrs Mummery, be it noted, was alive when this review appeared. He concludes his review by postulating that in certain important matters Mummery was insane.'

Whymper returned to the Alps four years after the accident, but was content, as Frank Smythe notes with regret, to wander about the valleys. His nerve was not affected by the accident, for he subsequently made some fine ascents in the Andes and Rockies, and he repeated his ascent of the Matterhorn by the route on which the accident took place but lacked the curiosity to complete the ascent of the Italian ridge on which all his earlier attempts were made. It is difficult to resist the conclusion that a mountain ceased to interest Whymper once he knew it had been climbed. In the whole course of his mountaineering career he climbed only seven peaks which had been previously ascended, and only five of whose previous ascent there was no doubt. No great mountaineer has been so little interested in mountains *as such*, apart from the opportunities which they offered of virgin ascents.

Whymper was indeed fundamentally an explorer. Whymper's expedition to the Andes, Frank Smythe wrote to me,

'marked a milestone in mountain exploration as distinct from mountain climbing. I was tremendously impressed by the way it was carried out. Whymper's food and equipment was absolutely first class and the whole organization was many years before its time. There was nothing so efficient for many years later.'

In 1901 he visited the Rockies. His chief guide on that occasion, the famous Christian Klucker, quarrelled with Whymper and attacked him in the book which Klucker wrote. Few men climbed with Whymper for more than one season. His guides, with the exception of Croz and Almer, disliked him, and he quarrelled not only with Klucker in the Rockies but with the Carrels who were his guides in the Andes.

'Whymper', writes Smythe, 'was a hard taskmaster to himself and to his guides; the gulf between him and them was absolute. He lived apart from his employees. He shared the same tent, but in other ways he might have been at the other end of the world. To his guides, rugged simple men, temperamental at times like children, he must have been totally unintelligible.'

On April 25, 1906, Whymper married Miss Edith Lewin, the ceremony being conducted by Canon J. McCormick who was by then Rector of St James's, Piccadilly. Whymper was forty-five years older than his wife, who obtained a judicial separation in 1910. Shortly after the separation Edith Whymper died. The Whympers had one child, a daughter, now Mrs E. Blandy, an enthusiastic mountaineer who has made many fine climbs in the Zermatt district. There were only two women, and perhaps only two human beings, for whom Whymper felt a really strong affection, his mother and Miss Charlotte Hanbury, whom he met when he was fifty-nine years of age, and who died a year after they met. Whymper died on September 13, 1911, at Chamonix.

Whymper was a friendless, and in many ways a pathetic man, and there was little, if anything, admirable about him excepting his mountaineering, but in spite of defects which I have not attempted to conceal, there was something great about the man. Many eminent mountaineers have contributed to the history of the Matterhorn by forcing new routes up its cliffs, but the Matterhorn remains Whymper's mountain, partly perhaps because he himself had something of the indomitable character of that great peak, with the result that we tend, as Geoffrey Winthrop Young rightly says, to identify him in our memory with the greatness of the Matterhorn. 'Through the attitudes of the protagonists' (of mountaineering), writes Young, 'he crashed with a rude personal vehemence that remains hopelessly individual.'

The first ascent of the Matterhorn.
July 13-14, 1865.

Several lines have been torn from this part of the "Livre des Strangers." These leaves
contained an account of the first ascent of the Matterhorn, of the accident which occurred
during the descent — in which Lord Francis Douglas, Mr Hadow, Mr Charles Hudson and
the guide Michel Croz lost their lives, and of the means which were taken to recover
their bodies. ———

This account was written for the information of the murderer-travellers who
visit Zermatt. It bore testimony to the courage of those who a lamentably perished,
to the devotion of Michel Croz; and, to the gallantry of the guides Franz Andermatten
and the brothers Lochmatter, who nobly volunteered to seek the bodies of those who
were lost, when not a single guide of Zermatt dared move, in face of threatened
excommunication by their priests ———

It spoke of the unrecompensing kindness of Madame and Monsieur Seiler. Other and more
valuable things — esteemed by Mons. Seiler, have also been stolen from his books ———
This account has been appropriated by some person unknown.

As the associate of those who lost their lives on the 14th of July, 1865, and of those
who outrageously performed an act of the highest courage, and as the friend of Mons.
Seiler I protest against these thefts. This book is the private property of Mons.
Seiler and no one has any more right to take a leaf from it than to
steal his money ———

Edward Whymper. Sept 1, 1864 —

[Photo: Kurverein Zermatt]

10. Edward Whymper's entry in the Monte Rosa Hotel guest book

[Photo: Kurverein Zermatt

11. Relics of the accident, now in the Zermatt Museum

2. Zermatt in Whymper's time

[Photo: Kurverein Zermat

13. The Taugwalders with American tourists

On re-reading his famous book I have again been deeply impressed by his courage and enterprise as a mountaineer. To the end he remained astonishingly tough. At the age of sixty-two he walked from Edinburgh to London, averaging fifty-five miles a day. I am also impressed by his superb self-confidence. He was not by origin a gentleman but he assumed, and rightly assumed, that he would be accepted by mountaineers on his own terms.

Whymper's first contact with English mountaineers was at Zermatt during his first visit to the Alps. The Alpine Club of that period was in the main recruited from those whom my brother Hugh Kingsmill described as 'mupples', that is, members of the upper middle class. Whymper was certainly not a mupple, for even his aspirates were uncertain, and at that time he had no great climbs to his credit to compensate for his lack of social qualifications. But this young man of twenty seems to have been serenely unconscious of the social gulf between him and the mupples of the Alpine Club. He gate-crashed into their society without realizing the existence of any barriers. 'The hotel', he wrote in his diary, 'is full of Alpine men, many of whom are very plucky fellows, and there are the usual number of bores.' T. W. Hinchliff, one of the leaders of this little society, offered to coach Whymper on the Riffelberg, 'which offer', he tells us, 'was gratefully accepted'. He was grateful, but not surprised by this condescension. Whymper had at least one characteristic of greatness, superb self-confidence. He was uninterested in and therefore uninfluenced by class distinctions.

His nephew describes him lunching at Anderton's Hotel in Fleet Street 'in a sweater that showed his bare bull-like neck to perfection; he seldom wore anything below the sweater'. He smoked the strongest possible shag, and the carpets, table cloths, upholstered chairs, etc., in his vicinity were frequently burnt full of holes. He invariably smoked in bed, 'and not only were his bedclothes soon riddled with holes but his own chest became scarred with hot ashes too'.

Scrambles amongst the Alps was first published in 1871 and its success was immediate. It was accepted both by mountaineers and the general public as an outstanding contribution to mountaineering literature. *Scrambles* owes much of its success to the wood engravings, and not one admirer of that book in a thousand gives credit to anybody but Whymper for the magnificent illustrations, by far the best artistic interpretation of mountain adventure at that time. Whymper tells us that he provided 'slight memoranda' in the shape of sketches but did not draw a single one of the illustrations on wood. James Mahonney drew on wood about fifty of Whymper's slight sketches and Whymper finished the engraving. Mahonney's work can usually be identified by, and only by, his monogram. 'I can't understand', Martin Conway once remarked to me, 'why Mahonney is only known to us because of *Scrambles*. His *Cannonade on the Matterhorn* is a remarkably effective bit of work.' Conway was the only mountaineer whom I have met who did not unconsciously give Whymper credit not only for the engravings but also for the drawings. Smythe told me that there are several sketches in Whymper's diary identical in character with those in *Scrambles*, and I am perplexed that so accomplished a draughtsman as Whymper undoubtedly was felt it necessary to employ not only Mahonney but also Cyrus Johnson to draw on wood from his own 'slight memoranda'.

Whymper had no talent for describing mountain scenery. He lacked Leslie Stephen's gift of selecting the epithet or simile which evokes a *particular* scene, and which *differentiates* one mountain view from another. His description of the view from the Matterhorn is a mere catalogue of peaks seen. There is no touch of nature mysticism in his writing. He did not seek in mountain worship a substitute for religion. He was primarily a sportsman concerned to solve a particular mountain problem, and certainly few mountaineers have been more successful in interpreting the romance of Alpine adventure. His writing is flavoured with a dry humour, very welcome by contrast with the depressing jocularity which was characteristic of so much of the Alpine literature at the period. His writing when sincere and simple is always effective and only fails when he is obviously writing for effect. At its worst his writing sinks to the low level of 'See yonder height! 'Tis far away—unbidden comes the word "Impossible!" "Not so", says the mountaineer. "The way is long, I know; it's difficult—it may be—dangerous. It's possible

I'm sure; I'll seek the way; take counsel of my brother mountaineers." '

But at its best Whymper's writing has a simplicity and directness which in his description of the Matterhorn tragedy challenges comparison with Thucydides. As long as men climb, *Scrambles Amongst the Alps* will continue to be read.

CHAPTER XII

Jean Antoine Carrel and the Italian Ridge

On July 14, 1865, Felice Giordano sent by express letter a triumphant report to Quintino Sella:

'Dear Quintino,
    'To-day with a good opera glass I saw Carrel on the summit . . . Whymper has gone to attempt the Matterhorn from the other side, but in vain, I believe.'

On July 15th triumphant joy gave way to bitter disillusion.

'Dear Quintino,
    'Yesterday was a bad day, and Whymper, after all, gained the victory over the unfortunate Carrel. Whymper, as I told you, was desperate, and seeing Carrel climbing the mountain, tried his fortune on the Zermatt slope. Everyone here, and Carrel above all, considered the ascent absolutely impossible on that side; so we were all easy in our minds . . .
    'I had, it is true, sent Carrel word of Whymper's proposed attempt, and had enjoined on him to get up at any cost, without loss of time to prepare the way, but my warning did not reach him in time, and moreover Carrel did not believe the ascent from the north to be possible. However, yesterday, as I saw some men on the Matterhorn, and was assured by everyone that they were our party, I sent off the telegram to you, bidding you come up. Poor Carrel, when he saw that he had been forestalled, had not the courage to proceed, and beat a retreat with his weapons and his baggage. He arrived here late this morning, and it was then that I sent off another telegram by express to stop you from

coming. As you see, although every man did his duty, it is a lost battle, and I am in great grief . . .

'At any rate, in order not to return ridiculous as well as unsuccessful, I think that we ought at least to plant our flag on the summit. I at once tried to organize a fresh expedition, but hitherto, with the exception of Carrel and another, I have not found any men of courage whom I can trust. Some others might, perhaps, be found if I paid them extravagantly, but I do not think it wise to go to such expense; and then, if their courage is deficient, there would be no certainty of success . . .

'Yesterday the Val Tournanche was already *en fête* thinking that we were victorious: to-day we were disillusioned. Poor Carrel is to be pitied, the more so as part of the delay was due to his idea that Whymper would not be able to ascend from Zermatt. I am trying to act like Terentius Varro after the battle of Cannae.'

If Carrel had not felt confident that Whymper would fail, he would have acted on Giordano's warning and wasted no time. He would certainly have left his bivouac at the earliest possible moment. Instead, Carrel and his companions did not leave until 6 a.m., and did not reach the foot of the final peak until 2 p.m., just in time to hear Whymper's victorious shouts on the summit.

It is said that Carrel and Maquignaz wished to continue but the other members of the party were reluctant to proceed. Carrel said, 'Either all or none', and started down. Carrel's judgment, and perhaps his nerve, failed him at this critical moment. Though Whymper had beaten him, the first ascent from Italy was still to be achieved. He could certainly have imposed his authority on his companions, and had they continued to the summit and returned in safety, their bloodless triumph might well have been deemed a greater victory than Whymper's tragic success.

Carrel returned to Breuil on the 14th, but it was not until the next day that he summoned up courage to report his failure to Giordano. 'Carrel', wrote Giordano in his letter to Sella, 'put the blame on his companions. They were very discouraged and feared that I might not wish to incur any further expense now that the battle had been lost.' Giordano resolved that the Italians should at least have the glory of making the first ascent of the Matterhorn from Italy. Carrel's companions refused to try again, in spite of all Giordano's efforts to convince them that both the honour and the interests of the Valtournanche guides were at stake.

The Abbé Gorret was the first to volunteer, and the party was completed by J. Augustin Meynet and J. Baptiste Bich, the servants of Favre, the innkeeper. Giordano was naturally most anxious to join the party, but Carrel declined to take him. He alleged that he could not undertake both to find a route to the summit and to look after a traveller. A poor decision, for Giordano was certainly as good a man on a mountain as either Meynet or Bich. Giordano insisted that Carrel should state in writing that he did not wish Giordano to be of the party. At the end of the day Giordano made a sad note in his pocket book:

'Walked a mile, suffering the pangs of disappointment. A very bad night with fever. Only one barometrical observation.'

Carrel's party started on Sunday the 16th, after hearing Mass at the chapel of Breuil. They pitched their tent at the usual bivouac place at the foot of the tower beyond Pic Tyndall. Carrel traversed to the west of the peak, hoping to reach the Zmutt ridge and complete the ascent by that ridge, but they had not proceeded very far on the west face before they were forced to retreat to the Breuil ridge, a traverse of considerable difficulty, in the course of which Gorret was wounded in the arm by a falling stone.

At last they reached the foot of the final tower. 'We stood', writes Gorret, 'in a place that was almost comfortable. Although it was not more than two yards wide, and the slope was one of seventy-five per cent, we gave it all kinds of pleasant names: the corridor, the gallery, the railroad, etc., etc.'

The last serious obstacle was a rocky cleft between them and the final easy section of the ridge. Carrel felt that it would be wiser to leave two of the party in order to help them up the wall of the cleft on their return. Gorret and Meynet sacrificed themselves, and shortly afterwards Carrel and Bich reached the summit.

At the Jomein, Giordano made the following entry in his diary:

'Splendid weather; at 9.30 saw Carrel and his men on the Shoulder, after that saw nothing more of them. Then much mist about the summit. Lifted a bit about 3.30, and we saw our flag on the western summit of the Matterhorn. The English flag looked like a black shawl lying on the snow, in the centre.'

Carrel's party spent another night on the mountain, and on their descent next day saw flags waving over the Jomein. Giordano's diary entry records the triumph: 'Great hilarity all day at the hotel and at Breuil, bonfires and songs. Amid the rejoicing I alone was sad: I had not personally climbed the Matterhorn.'

At Valtournanche they sang

> 'Vive le Monsieur Italien
> Qui a vaincu le Mont Cervin!'

Giordano was called back to Turin by business, and from Turin he wrote to Sella:

'I wished to tell you that, if you wish, you may still climb the Matterhorn and gain some honour as the first "Monsieur" to do it from the Italian side. So I have had the tent and some ropes left up there.

'Although we have been forestalled by Whymper, the victory from a practical point of view is ours, because we have now proved that the peak is accessible on our side, while it does not seem as if any other ascent would be attempted in a hurry from Zermatt. Poor Whymper is overcome by his ephemeral victory, while the Val Tournanche is full of joy at the sight of the three-coloured flag calmly waving on the lofty peak. You could still make scientific geological and barometrical observations up there; the peak might still be considered as virgin from this point of view, and we should thus give a solemn proof of the feasibility of the route on the Italian side, and of our calm perseverance in the face of the tragic upshot of the Zermatt ascent.'

Thirty-five years later Carrel, who was then in his sixty-second year, died on the Italian ridge which he had been the first to attack and the first to climb. On August 23, 1890, Leone Sinigaglia engaged Carrel for a traverse of the Matterhorn. They were caught by bad weather in the Italian hut where they spent two nights. Sinigaglia noticed that Carrel was unwell, but provisions were running out and it was decided to descend. The rocks were partially buried in snow and, where exposed, were covered by a thin film of ice. Carrel insisted on leading, and fought his way down towards safety, undaunted by a blinding snowstorm. Fourteen hours after leaving the hut they were still on the rocks, but Carrel refused to allow another guide to relieve him.

No sooner had they reached easy ground than Carrel collapsed. 'We tried to lift him,' wrote Sinigaglia, 'but it was impossible. He was getting stiff. We stooped down and asked him if he wished to commend his soul to God. With a last effort he answered, "Yes", and then fell on his back, dead, upon the snow.'

During his lifetime many guides of Breuil resented Carrel's unchallenged supremacy, but none questioned his greatness. Years later a climber paused before the cross which was erected near the point where Carrel died, and remarked to the son of Carrel's greatest rival, 'So that is where Carrel fell'.

'Carrel did not fall', came the indignant reply. 'Carrel died.'

NOTE

Leone Sinigaglia, who was born at Turin on August 14, 1863, was distinguished not only as a mountaineer—the book in which he describes his Dolomite climbs has been translated into English—but also as a musician and as the man who did most to preserve the traditional folk-songs of Piedmont.

In the late autumn of 1943 he spent a night at San Remigio with my friend Count Aldo Bonacossa, a distinguished mountaineer and an honorary member of the Alpine Club, whose wife, Countess Bonacossa, was known as the Mother of the Partisans. It was a great joy and surprise for Sinigaglia to meet a mountaineer who knew all about his Dolomite climbs, and thus to escape for a few hours from the tragedy of Italy's involvement in a war in alliance with the Nazis whom both men detested. The next night Sinigaglia failed to cross the frontier, returned to Turin and hid in a hospital. In the spring of 1944 he was discovered by the Nazis and was to have been sent to Germany next day. Knowing full well what awaited him there, he died of a heart attack on May 14, 1944.

4. The younger Taugwalder in later years

15. Professor John Tyndall

CHAPTER XIII

Some Early Ascents

Two months after the first ascent of the Matterhorn, a famous German mountaineer, Dr Paul Güssfeldt, arrived in Zermatt determined to climb the Matterhorn, but the tragedy of the first ascent had had a demoralising effect on the local guides, of whom only the elder Taugwalder was prepared to consider the ascent, and even Taugwalder refused to repeat the route from Zermatt. 'He was', wrote Güssfeldt, 'too shaken by the disaster in which he had so narrowly escaped death that long negotiations and substantial offers were necessary to persuade him and his son to attempt once more this formidable enterprise.' And even so, Taugwalder preferred to attempt the Matterhorn from Breuil than by the route which he already knew. They accordingly crossed the Théodule to Breuil but their attempt on the Matterhorn failed. It was not until August 9, 1868, that Dr Güssfeldt finally succeeded in climbing the Matterhorn from Zermatt with Peter Knubel and Joseph Marie Lochmatter of St Niklaus, descending by the same Zermatt route. Güssfeldt's was the tenth ascent of the Matterhorn.

The second ascent of the Matterhorn, and the first from Breuil, has been described in Chapter XI. The third ascent was made on August 13-15, 1867, by F. Craufurd Grove with the guides J. A. Carrel, Solomon Meynet and J. B. Bich.

'Our route was identical', wrote Craufurd Grove in an account written for Whymper, 'with that which they (Carrel's party on the first ascent from Italy) followed in their descent when, as will be seen, they struck out on one part of the mountain a different line from that which they had taken in ascending.'[1]

Craufurd Grove was the first amateur to ascend the Matter-

[1] *Scrambles*, p. 406.

horn since the accident, and the inhabitants of the Valtour-nanche were delighted that the ascent had been made from Breuil.

'Some of them', writes Whymper, 'were by no means well pleased that J. A. Carrel was so much regarded. They feared, perhaps, that he would acquire the monopoly of the mountain. Just a month after Mr Grove's ascent, six Valtournanchians set out to see whether they could not learn the route, and so come in for a share of the good things which were expected to arrive.'[1]

The six in question were three Maquignaz brothers, Jean Joseph, Jean Pierre and Victor, the cousins César Carrel, described by Whymper as 'my old guide', Jean Baptiste Carrel, and a daughter of the last named, Félicité, aged eighteen.

They left Breuil at 5 a.m. on September 12, 1867, and reached the little hut, 'Refuge de la Cravate', at 3 p.m. where they spent the night. They left at 7 a.m. next morning, leaving J. B. Carrel behind, and proceeded along the shoulder to the final peak, passing the cleft which had stopped Bennen on Tyndall's attempt, and clambered up easy rocks on the other side to the base of the final precipice. One of the main objectives of this expedition was to find a purely Italian route to the summit which at no point traversed on to the Swiss north face.

Jean Joseph Maquignaz considered that the difficulties would prove too great for a large party and decided that his sole com-panion on the final section should be his brother Pierre. The point where the rest of the party stopped was named Col Félicité by William Leighton Jordan on his ascent twenty days later (October 2nd).

The Maquignaz brothers then climbed with great difficulty an abrupt cliff the ascent of which is now facilitated by a ladder. On the snows of the summit they planted a flag and a medal of the Madonna.

'It is', writes Charles Gos, 'interesting to note that this route was that which Abbé Gorret had suggested. He had favoured the direct attack instead of the traverse on to the Zmutt face.'[2]

On their descent they attached a rope at the most dangerous

[1] *Scrambles*, p. 407.
[2] *Le Cervin*, Tome 1, p. 239.

point which they left in position, and which is referred to in Tyndall's account of the first traverse of the Matterhorn from Italy to Switzerland. Leighton Jordan had used this rope on his ascent and been worried by doubts of its durability. He therefore offered to finance replacing it by a rope ladder, and two years later this ladder was placed in position on August 27, 1869, in the course of an ascent by R. L. Heathcote with the guides Jean Joseph, Jean Pierre, Victor and Emmanuel Maquignaz.

Whymper's comment on this brilliant climb does not err on the side of generosity.

'It should be observed', he writes, 'that ropes had been fixed, by J. A. Carrel and others, over *all* the difficult parts of the mountain as high as the shoulder, *before* the ascent of these persons. This explains the facility with which they moved over ground which had been found very trying in earlier times. The young woman declared that the ascent (as far as she went) was a trifle, or used words to that effect; if she had tried to get to the same height before 1862 she would probably have been of a different opinion.'[1]

It was to Canon Carrel that Félicité Carrel, in reply to his questions, described her impressions of the climb. It had been, she said, less difficult than she expected, none the less the Matterhorn was very high and the climb was very long, and a woman ought not to climb in a long dress. Those who could not climb or who could not without anxiety look at precipitous cliffs without worrying should not attempt the Matterhorn and, finally, the money paid to the guides was well earned.

On October 2, 1867, Leighton Jordan with the guides Jean Joseph and Jean Pierre Maquignaz and Victor Maquignaz, as porter, climbed the Matterhorn from Breuil, following the direct route up the final peak, first achieved by his own guides a few days earlier.

They then descended towards Zermatt by the usual Swiss route until they reached a point where they had been stopped by bad weather three weeks earlier. Instead of continuing down to Zermatt, as they could easily have done, they decided to return to the summit, spend a second night in the 'Refuge de la

[1] *Scrambles*, p. 409.

Cravate' and cross the mountain next day to Zermatt. Had they not been completely confident that the good weather would continue, they would have completed the descent to Zermatt. Even so their decision to postpone the traverse till next day admits of no really convincing explanation. Next day the weather broke and Jordan lost the chance of being the first to turn the Matterhorn into a pass. He tried to console himself with the reflection that he was the only man who had climbed and descended every foot of both the Italian and the Swiss routes, but I think Captain J. P. Farrar was too generous in giving Jordan the credit of making what Farrar called the first *virtual* traverse of the Matterhorn, the complete ascent from Breuil and the descent of the two sections of the Swiss route on two different occasions. If Jordan had continued the descent on the Swiss side, he would have had the honour of being the first to follow the Swiss route since the first ascent.

It was not until rather more than three years after the first ascent that the Matterhorn was again climbed from Zermatt, though four ascents had been made by then from Breuil.

Julius Marshall Elliott, who made the second ascent from Zermatt, was born at Brighton on October 24, 1841. His father, the Rev. Henry Venn Elliott, who was a first cousin of Leslie Stephen's mother, a Miss Venn. Julius Elliott who was educated at Brighton College and Trinity College Cambridge, was ordained in 1865, and succeeded his father at St. Mary's Chapel, Brighton. He was an ardent walker in the Lake District, and discovered in 1864, with A. J. Butler, the now usual route up the Pillar.

Early in July 1868 Dr W. A. B. Coolidge met Elliott in the Gleckstein cave on the Wetterhorn. 'In the course of conversation', wrote Coolidge, 'Mr. Elliott revealed, almost under the seal of confession, his strong desire, even his fixed intention, to attempt the Matterhorn from the Swiss side.' The story of that successful attempt was originally written for *The Field* and a revised version was published in the *Alpine Journal*, Vol. XXVIII.

After climbing the Dom, Elliott sounded his guide, Franz Biener, on the subject of the Matterhorn:

'His answer was very touching to me. As far as I can recollect, it was this: —"Dear sir, I love you well. I know you are strong and sure of foot, and I should like to go with you everywhere. But my mother—if we should slip and fall, it would be sad for me, and sad for her." It was unanswerable. I turned the subject and said, "Well, will you try the Weisshorn? Do you think it can be done now; and do you think I am up to it?" *"Ja wohl, Herr,"* sounded out with a full and round voice, very different from the previous words. So off we went and did the Weisshorn. This settled the question in my mind, that, come what might, I would try the Matterhorn, weather being good.'

Elliott made one more effort to persuade Biener to accompany him. Biener agreed to ask his mother.

'In the afternoon he returned with a sad and wistful look and said, "No, sir; I cannot go. My mother cried much when I spoke of it, and said, 'Do not go, Franz, I entreat thee, do not go.'" I at once responded, "That settles the question; don't go on any account; you have done quite right to make that resolve". And so it happened that I found myself, on July 24, 1868, without my own trusty guide, making arrangements with two men who knew nothing of me, and of whom I knew nothing, who had not been up the Matterhorn or any really dangerous mountain, and of whose capacity to render help when wanted my opinion did not increase upon experience.'

One of these guides, father of the famous Franz Lochmatter, was Joseph Marie Lochmatter, who was killed on the Dent Blanche in 1882 with his eldest son and with Mr. W. E. Gabbett. Peter Knubel was a first class guide. Elliott's aspersions on his guides shocked many members of the Alpine Club, among them Whymper. Elliott's long letter to a friend of his, Mr. Wood, was first published in *The Field* in 1910, long after Elliott's death. The Editor referred the letter to Whymper.

'Mr. Whymper', wrote the Editor, 'entirely dissociates himself from the opinion expressed by Mr. Elliott concerning the experience and capabilities of the guides, for Lochmatter was a competent mountaineer, and Peter Knubel, says Mr. Whymper, "is still alive, and in working order at seventy-five years of age, after having made more than a hundred ascents of the Matterhorn." '

Elliott was not impressed by the difficulties of the climb. The most difficult part is a steep pitch above the shoulder and not far from the summit, 'a formidable barrier of steep rock, which runs right across the face of the mountain. This is undoubtedly the chief difficulty on this side, but I cannot say that it struck me as anything remarkable.'

'It will be seen,' commented the Editor of the *Alpine Journal* who reprinted this account in 1914,[1] 'that Mr. Elliott's estimate of the difficulty corresponds very closely with the views of today.'

'I think my first impressions', wrote Elliott, 'after the first wild delight of finding myself at the top, were those of caution and doubt, whispered, as by an enemy, "Yes: but you are not down safe yet". But never came there a moment's apprehension. A passing shudder there was as I saw the place where "they" fell, and the hopelessness of arresting such a fall.'

Elliott's first account of this climb, a private letter to his friend, Mr. Wood, was far franker than the account published in 1914 in the *Alpine Journal*. Here is his description of his reception in Zermatt.

'Tired out with waiting for the guides, who were perpetually stopping to eat or rest, I reached Zermatt at 4.23, twelve hours and eight minutes from the start, the guides, half an hour afterwards. I fortunately came down long before anyone expected me, and so avoided recognition. I learned afterwards that the whole of Zermatt had turned out to look at us on the top. Breakfast was neglected and people went mad on the spot, more especially because the climber was unknown to fame, and the ascent almost wholly unexpected. At dinner Mr Seiler sent me in a bottle of champagne with his compliments, and Mme Seiler a bouquet, very tastefully got up; a discharge of improvised cannon completed the absurdity.'

[1] Vol. XXVIII, p. 286.

Elliott was killed on the Schreckhorn on July 27, 1869. The party had reached the foot of the final arête, which, at that time and for many years after, was gained by ascending a steep slope of hard snow or ice, since called 'Elliott's Wängli'. The party was, it is stated on Elliott's own insistence,[1] not roped.

'In making a spring from the ice slope to the rocks which the leader had gained, Elliott missed his footing and slid, at first slowly, down the slope on the Lauteraar side and was killed. But for losing his axe, Biener is of opinion that he would certainly have stopped himself.'

On July 20, 1867, Tyndall arrived in Breuil with an Oberland guide, and met J. A. Carrel with a view to engaging him for an attempt on the Matterhorn. Carrel by then had made the first ascent of the Matterhorn from Breuil and, to quote Tyndall,

'had naturally and deservedly grown in his own estimation. But I was discomforted by the form his self-consciousness assumed. His demands were exorbitant and he also objected to the excellent company of Christian Michel. In fact my friend Carrel was no longer a reasonable man. I believe he afterwards felt ashamed of himself.'

Charles Gos quotes some reflections of Canon Carrel on this melancholy incident.[2]

'It was M. Tyndall who on July 28th 1862 worked out, so to speak, the route up Mont Cervin. It was he who arranged for a rope to be fixed on the most difficult section, and he was the first to arrive on the shoulder which now bears his name, Pic Tyndall. He had also contributed fifty francs to the construction of a refuge. He certainly deserved some consideration. Journalists expressed their indigation.[3] Many people who spoke or who wrote to me were indignant. For my part I took the opportunity publicly to express my sympathy with M. Tyndall and to make clear how grieved I had been.'

Tyndall in a letter from London, dated October 22, 1867,

[1] See, however, *A Century of Mountaineering*, pp. 49-50.
[2] *Le Cervin* 1, p. 255.
[3] *Feuille d'Aosta*, September 3rd, No. 36.

stated that he had been faced by the demand to take four guides, each of whom was to be paid 150 francs, a grand total of 600 francs. Not being an economist I will not attempt to estimate the corresponding sum in modern purchasing power. A distinguished Italian who was personally connected with some of the Italian pioneers, remarked to me that J. A. Carrel's chief fault was that he was too fond of money.

On Tuesday, July 21, 1868, Tyndall met by arrangement Canon Carrel, who as we have seen was aware of the fact that Tyndall was dissatisfied with J. A. Carrel's behaviour the previous year.

'He had written to me during the winter, stating that two new men had scaled the Matterhorn, and that they were ready to accompany me anywhere ... At Val Tournanche I saw a maiden niece of the Chanoine who had gone high up the Matterhorn,[1] and who, had the wind not assailed her petticoats too roughly, might, it was said, have reached the top. I can believe it. Her wrist was like a weaver's beam and her frame seemed a mass of potential energy. The Chanoine had recommended to me as guides the brothers Joseph and Pierre Maquignaz of Val Tournanche, his praises of Joseph as a man of unshaken coolness, courage, and capacity as a climber being particularly strong ... Carrel was at Breuil, looking very dark; Bich petitioned for a porter's post, blaming Carrel bitterly for his greed in the previous year.'

The weather broke on Thursday but appeared to improve on Friday.

'I enquired of my companion whether, in the event of the day being fine, he would be ready to start on Sunday. His answer was a prompt negative. In Val Tournanche, he said, they always "sanctified the Sunday". I mentioned Bennen, my pious Catholic guide, whom I permitted and encouraged to attend his mass on all possible occasions, but who, nevertheless, always yielded without a murmur to the demands of the weather. The reasoning had its effect. On Saturday Maquignaz saw his confessor, and arranged with him to have a mass at 2 a.m. on Sunday; after

[1] See p. 82.

which, unshaded by the sense of duties unperformed, he would commence the ascent. The claims of religion being thus met, the point of next importance, that of money, was set at rest by my immediate acceptance of the tariff published by the Chanoine Carrel.'

They started the climb on July 26th and spent the night in the hut which had been built on an almost horizontal ledge, always loaded with snow, which, from its resemblance to a white necktie, has been called the *Cravate*. They left the hut just after six and arrived on the summit at shortly before eleven. They were surprised to discover footmarks in the snow which, as they subsequently learned, were those of Elliott's party which had climbed the Matterhorn two days before.

Tyndall was resolved to be the first to turn the Matterhorn into a pass by ascending from Breuil and descending to Zermatt. The summit slope 'was in the worst possible condition'. There was about fifteen inches of new snow on the rocks.

'In treading it we came immediately upon the rock, which in most cases was too smooth to furnish either prop or purchase. It was on this slope that the Matterhorn catastrophe occurred: it is on this slope that other catastrophes will occur, if ever this mountain should become fashionable. Joseph Maquignaz was the leader of our little party, and a brave, cool, and competent leader he proved himself to be. He was silent, save when he answered his brother's anxious and oft-repeated question, "Es-tu bien placé, Joseph?" Along with being perfectly cool and brave, he seemed to be perfectly truthful. He did not pretend to be *bien placé* nor avow a power of holding which he did not possess.'

All their difficulties were over when they reached the shoulder. but they lost their way in the darkness below the Hörnli and only reached Zermatt between one and two on the morning of July 28th.

I am indebted to Whymper's list of the early ascents of the Matterhorn for the dates of this memorable expedition. It is odd that Tyndall, an eminent scientist and as such, one might imagine, more precise in reporting dates than ordinary folk, does

not give the date of this climb from the beginning to the end of
Chapter XXIV of *Hours of Exercise in the Alps* in which the
climb is described.

On August 2nd - 3rd of the same year two Genevese, Francois
Thioly and O. Hoiler, traversed the Matterhorn from Zermatt
to Breuil. They had great difficulty in finding a guide willing to
accompany them. Hoiler was wearing *'un affreux chapeau de
buchilles de 50 centimes . . . vouloir monter le Cervin avec ce
couvre-chef semblait une act de folie.*[1] Unfortunately Hoiler,
who was a member of the Cercle des Vieux-Grenadiers de
Genève, had vowed in the presence of his fellow-members of this
club that he would climb the Matterhorn in this deplorable hat,
and nothing would persuade him to exchange it for more
convenable headgear. The Zermatt guides not unreasonably felt
that a man who proposed to wear such a hat on the Matterhorn
could not be taken seriously as a climber. Hence their refusal to
accept an engagement.

Luckily for Thiolly and Hoiler they ran into the Maquignaz
brothers who had just traversed the Matterhorn with Tyndall,
and who were delighted to earn a good fee by repeating the
traverse in the opposite direction, which was successfully accomplished by Thioly and Hoiler and the notorious hat on
August 3-4, 1868.

[1] *Le Cervin* by Charles Gos. Tome I, p. 274.

CHAPTER XIV

The First Ascent by a Woman

The first ascent of the Matterhorn by a woman was Lucy Walker's ascent of the Matterhorn on July 20, 1871, and I must begin by acknowledging my indebtedness to a chapter on Lucy Walker in a book which is as readable as it is informative, *They came to the Hills* by that gifted French author, Dr Claire Eliane Engel.[1]

Lucy Walker was the daughter and sister of mountaineers. Her father, Francis Walker, was born in 1808. In 1825 he climbed up to the Théodule at a time when that long and easy walk was still deemed a serious mountain expedition. Later he climbed many peaks with his son Horace, and with his daughter Lucy. The Walkers were dealers in lead in Liverpool. Horace Walker was born in Calcutta, educated by a private tutor in Switzerland and joined his father's business at the age of nineteen years.

In 1858 Francis Walker decided to revisit the Théodule, his first mountain expedition, with his son. Somebody suggested that Lucy should join them, an invitation which she gladly accepted. Lucy decided that she would wear her old white print dress, which achieved fame when she wore it some years later during her famous ascent of the Matterhorn.

It was on the Théodule that Lucy first suspected that mountains and mountaineering were to prove the dominant interest of her life. An easy walk up the Monte Moro reinforced this conviction. Thereafter Lucy was admitted as a fully qualified member of the Walker team.

In 1862 she climbed the Oberaarhorn and Finsteraarhorn with her brother Horace, and the Alphubel, Monte Rosa, and Mont

[1] George Allen and Unwin Ltd.

Blanc by the Aiguille du Goûter, with her father. In 1863 the united Walker team, Francis, Horace and Lucy, climbed the Zumsteinspitze. In 1864 the family were divided. Horace joined Whymper for a famous campaign in the Dauphiné, in the course of which Whymper and Walker made the first ascent of the Pointe des Ecrins. Whymper then returned to Zermatt to renew his assaults on the Matterhorn. Horace Walker joined his father and Lucy, who had just climbed the Grivola. After the family team had climbed the Combin, they proceeded to Zermatt, where Lucy and her father climbed the Rimpfischhorn with A. W. Moore and then moved to Bel Alp, from which they ascended the Aletschhorn. A few days later, the Walker team made the first ascent of the Balmhorn, probably the only occasion when a father, son and daughter have made the first ascent of a big peak. By the time Lucy retired from mountaineering, she had climbed the great majority of the more famous Swiss and Savoy peaks and many summits in Bavaria and in the Dolomites. Her guide on almost all these climbs was the famous Melchior Anderegg.

'According to notes', writes Dr Engel, 'which have been given me by Mr Solly, a friend of the Walkers, she was in every other respect (than mountaineering) the perfect Victorian young lady. She was not an athlete and her greatest asset when climbing was her unflinching will-power. She did not ride or fish or take walking tours, which were the accepted forms of exertion for girls at that time. She indulged in no outdoor recreation but croquet. For the rest, she was an expert needlewoman, read widely in several languages, took an active part in the social life of Liverpool and was a charming hostess and devoted friend. Yet there was nothing lackadaisical about her climbs. She decided to conquer the highest and most difficult peaks and usually succeeded.'

In a famous illustration in *Scrambles*, 'The Club-Room of Zermatt in 1864', Whymper has given us a portrait of Francis Walker, sitting just behind Leslie Stephen, and Lucy is generally supposed to be the original of the tall girl standing in the door of the Monte Rosa Hotel, but Whymper, in the key to this illustration, most unchivalrously offers no clue to her identity.

Horace Walker, who is unaccountably omitted, was president of the Alpine Club from 1890 to 1893 and died in 1908.

On July 17, 1871, Lucy ascended the Weisshorn and four days later, on July 21st, she made the nineteenth ascent of the Matterhorn and the first by a woman. She was accompanied by her father, who was then already sixty-five years of age, and Frederick Gardiner (vice-president of the Alpine Club, 1896-8). Her guides were Melchior and Heinrich Anderegg, Peter Knubel and Peter Perren.

On August 26th, five weeks after this memorable achievement, *Punch* paid her a tribute in a poem entitled *A Climbing Girl*:

> A lady has clomb to the Matterhorn's summit
> Which almost like a monument points to the sky;
> Steep not very much less than the string of a plummet
> Suspended, which nothing can scale but a fly.
> This lady has likewise ascended the Weisshorn
> And, what's a great deal more, descended it, too,
> Feet foremost; which seeing it might be named Icehorn
> So slippery 'tis, no small thing is to do—
> No glacier can baffle, no precipice balk her,
> No peak rise above her, however sublime,
> Give three times three cheers for intrepid Miss Walker.
> I say, my boys, doesn't she know how to climb!

Long after Lucy ceased to climb she continued to visit the Alps and, in spite of her unassuming modesty, was inevitably the 'First Lady' on arriving at any Alpine centre. She was the second president of the Ladies' Alpine Club, the first being the founder, Mrs Aubrey Le Blond, a pioneer of winter mountaineering. She succeeded Mrs Le Blond in 1912, and by then she was already seventy-seven years of age and an invalid who seldom left her home in Liverpool. But in 1913 at the cost of a great effort she attended the annual dinner in London. 'Her after-dinner speech', writes Dr Engel, 'was spirited and racy. She had to be helped to her feet by two of her old climbing companions but she then spoke with vigour and enjoyment. She alluded to her ascent of the Matterhorn and to the outfit she wore on that occasion, the celebrated "white print dress". One of the members present, Miss Western, apropos of this meeting, wrote to me: "She was so charming to us all and seemed so pleased, and I might say so touched that younger climbers wanted to do her honour". After ninety-eight great ascents in the course of her life, Miss Walker when eighty still retained the old pleasant unassuming personality which had been her characteristic feature in the days when she opened a new path for women.'

Lucy Walker died at the age of eighty-one in 1916.

CHAPTER XV

The First Guideless Ascent

On July 23, 1876, three members of the Alpine Club, A. Cust, A. H. Cawood and J. B. Colgrove, made the first guideless ascent of the Matterhorn. Before describing an achievement which attracted at the time comments ranging from discerning praise to uncritical abuse, it is relevant to review the evolution in the attitude of the Alpine Club to guideless climbing.

In 1870 F. C. Grove read a paper to the Alpine Club on a book which had recently been published, *The High Alps Without Guides*, by the Rev. A. G. Girdlestone. Girdlestone was an enterprising but incompetent climber, and his misadventures on comparatively easy expeditions provided the critics of guideless climbing with ammunition. At the conclusion of Grove's paper 'it was agreed without a single dissentient that it is highly desirable that it should be known to be the settled opinion of the Alpine Club that whilst the danger may be reduced to an insignificant amount by proper care, the neglect to take guides on difficult expeditions, and especially the neglect to take them when the party is not exclusively composed of practised mountaineers, is totally unjustifiable and calculated to produce the most lamentable results'.

Now Grove had described the Wetterhorn, which Girdlestone climbed, as 'very difficult', and the resolution condemning 'the neglect to take guides on difficult expeditions' was, in effect, the condemnation of guideless climbing except on very easy mountains. John Ball, Leslie Stephen, Alfred Wills and Douglas Freshfield all voted for this bizarre resolution, in spite of the fact that members of the Alpine Club had already initiated guideless climbing and achieved outstanding successes, which should surely have had more influence on the club than Girdlestone's failures on comparatively easy mountains.

Hudson, E. S. Kennedy, C. Ainslie and C. and J. G. Smyth had made guideless ascents of the Klein Matterhorn and Breithorn, and the first guideless ascent of Mont Blanc (and also the first ascent from St Gervais), as early as 1855. Even more remarkable were the guideless ascents of the three brothers A. T., S. S. and C. S. Parker. In 1860 they crossed the Strahlegg and Schwarzberg Weissthor and made the first attempt on the Matterhorn from Zermatt. In 1865 they made a guideless ascent of the Finsteraarhorn.

What was particularly deplorable about the resolution of 1870 condemning guideless climbing was the fact that it ignored the great role which members of the club had played in pioneering the finest of all forms of mountaineering. Two years after the passing of this resolution, John Stogdon, a famous Harrow master, and the Rev. Arthur Fairbanks made guideless ascents of the Gross Nesthorn and Aletschhorn but did not dare to publish accounts of their expeditions for fear of provoking the orthodox. Many of the happiest hours which I spent during my schooldays at Harrow were with John Stogdon, inducing him to reminisce about the pioneering period. He was one of the most lovable of men. 'You have little idea', he once remarked to me, 'of the awe with which climbers were regarded in the 'seventies. The prestige of even mediocre mountaineers in those days was hardly less than that of a golf champion today.'

Some of these mountaineers were intellectuals who had made no mark at school in competitive sports but who had the enterprise to perceive the possibilities of this new sport, mountaineering, and the necessary stamina and courage. It was, perhaps, a new and not unwelcome experience for scholars who had been derided as 'saps' while at school, to be chided by their female friends for their reckless courage in facing the perils of the Alps. And it was perhaps not surprising that those who could not have led a guideless party up a second-class peak should react without great enthusiasm to a development which threatened to divide mountaineers into a guideless élite and a guided proletariat.

Guideless mountaineering developed earlier and was more widely practised among the Germans than among our own

16. Miss Lucy Walker

17. The North Face (air photo)

[Photo: Swissair

people. Herr Wilhelm Lehner in his monumental work *Die Eroberung der Alpen* explains this contrast by the contrast between the average income of the British and of the German mountaineers. The British were in the main well-to-do and could afford guides, whereas mountaineering in Germany was the sport of the middle classes and above all of young university students. Few Germans could afford to pay for guides.

Again, 'the Englishmen came to the Alps as fully developed master men (*fertige Herrenmenschen*). They were financially independent and in a position to develop their personalities by free choice of a career. The German, on the other hand, came from a narrow circle, and was forced to devote himself throughout his life to a restricted calling . . . Fully conscious of his "Herrentum", the Anglo-Saxon could afford to disregard his dependance on guides. The German was attracted by guideless climbing because he found in it the freedom which he missed elsewhere, the awakening of his dormant sense of mastery.'[1]

The paper which Cust read before the Alpine Club[2] after the first guideless ascent of the Matterhorn is mainly interesting for the introductory apologia for guideless climbing. The climb was, of course, attacked in the Press. 'A solitary instance of sense in an autumn article in the *Daily News* may perhaps', writes Cust, 'have been due to the employment of the ordinary writers of that paper in Bulgaria.'

Cust began by drawing attention to certain developments which, in his view, would tend to increase the number of guideless climbers. There had been a sharp increase in the number of mountaineers, but the number of 'really good guides remained strictly limited, and the competition between the old aristocracy of the Alps, to use metaphorical language, and the moneyed upstarts has resulted in a rise of prices . . . Proud as we have reason to be of the exploits of our countrymen, we must still acknowledge the truth that they, to except a few well-to-do individuals from other countries, have for years had a monopoly of the services of the competent guides.'

Cust's next point was that 'real Mountaineers' could only

---

[1] I have discussed this question at greater length in Chapter IX ('Portrait of a Club') of my book *Switzerland and the English*.

[2] Reprinted in Volume VIII, pp. 242-56.

differentiate themselves from 'the present shoals of professing climbers' by dispensing with guides.

'The one requisite for success in the case of a young man of good health and walking powers who wishes to try the excitement of, or get a name for, the loftiest climbing, is money. Cricket is a thing that is admitted by all to need acquired skill; a man can buy his mountaineering as he can his yachting; but for all that there are yachtsmen and yachtsmen.'

'Nothing', Cust generously concedes, 'can be more innocent, nay more commendable, in the ordinary and peaceful visitor to Switzerland, of either sex, than getting an introduction to the upper ice-world by means of a little casual mountain climbing. I should be the first to recommend it to my friends—the last to depreciate their success. Such gentle and modest persons are more than welcome to a diversion which adds charm to their society.'

Cust then dealt effectively with the objection that their guideless ascent of the Matterhorn might encourage less competent climbers to follow their example with disastrous results, and quotes with good humour some comments on the development of guideless climbing which were not wholly divorced from reality.

'A writer in the *Era*,' he writes, 'supplies the true origin of our expedition. After showing "how musty University dons leave their books and their mathematical instruments to show that in Switzerland there is 'life in the old dog yet' ", and that "the popularity of Alpine climbing has directly suggested a new excitement", he refers to our ascent. "Here", says he, "we have the new excitement. As it was found that University rooms and public school-houses and barristers' chambers echoed no more with the marvellous history of the feats of so-and-so . . . it became necessary to do a deed of exceptional daring. Accordingly, to go up mountains without guides was immediately decided upon!'

Cawood and Colgrove spent the day before the actual climb on an expedition to find the old club hut, which was situated at a height of 12,510 feet above the sea, and about 1,600 feet above the new hut which is the point where the actual climb begins. The hut, which was not visible till the climber arrived within a few minutes of it, was not too easy to find.

They left Zermatt next day at 11.15 a.m. with porters. 'During the ascent Colgrove kept in front to show the porters their real character, and the fact of our knowledge of the route.' Once arrived at the hut the porters deposited their loads and returned to Zermatt.

Cust, Cawood and Colgrove left the hut next morning at 4 a.m. and reached the shoulder at 6 a.m. where they halted for three-quarters of an hour. They experienced no difficulty on the remainder of the ascent, the steeper pitches having already been provided with fixed chains. There were no incidents on the descent. They reached Zermatt at 9.30 p.m.

'A friendly welcome awaited us; we had been traced down to the hut by the watchers good M. Seiler had told off to keep us in sight all day. Every servant on the staircase had his word of greeting. Doctor Porges, who had argued us down by the hour the night before our start, and stoutly maintained the improbability of our reaching the top, now recanted with fervour; unfortunately he had forgotten to order the brass band and cannon which he had said should celebrate our triumph!'

CHAPTER XVI

The First Winter Ascent

The first winter ascent of the Matterhorn was made by Vittorio Sella. He was born on August 28, 1859, the son of a textile manufacturer of Biella, and the nephew of Quintino Sella, the great statesman of the Risorgimento and the founder of the Italian Alpine Club, whose statue can be seen at Biella and who was, as we have seen, so actively concerned in the attempt to forestall Whymper and secure for Italy the glory of the first ascent of the Matterhorn.

Vittorio's father died when he was young and it was his famous uncle, Quintino Sella, who assumed responsibility for his education. Vittorio Sella was not the only nephew who was fired by his uncle's passion for mountaineering, for Guido Rey, whose conquest of the Furggen ridge is described in Chapter XVIII was also a nephew of Quintino.

Vittorio Sella's father, Venanzio, was a pioneer photographer, and wrote the first text book on photography to be published in Italy.

Vittorio was a pioneer of mountain photography. His first success was a panorama from the summit of Mont Mars near Biella. The camera weighed nearly forty pounds, the plates over two pounds each. Every plate had to be sensitized in a tent before being exposed, and basins, bottles and canvas buckets had to be carried to the summit of peaks, among them Mont Blanc, from which he photographed the panorama. His plates measured twelve by fourteen inches. The total weight of camera, tripod, slides and photographic equipment which Sella took with him on his famous expeditions to the Caucasus was 270 pounds.

Sella's photograph library, plates and prints are today housed in the Sella Institute at Biella. There is a photograph of the historic camera and of his descendant, Lodovico Sella, facing page 186 of A *Century of Mountaineering*.

Sella was a pioneer not only of mountain photography but also of winter mountaineering. He made two attempts on the Matterhorn during the course of February 1882. In March he returned to Breuil, and on March 16th he left Breuil at 11 p.m. with Louis, J. A. and Baptiste Carrel. They climbed by lantern light to the foot of the Great Tower, which they reached as dawn broke.

'The sky was serene,' writes Sella, 'all the tones were cold, but warm towards the west. A beautiful day was beginning. The prospect of at last conquering this majestic mountain filled me with a sentiment of profound satisfaction and moral energy. I have seldom felt so strong physically, or so alert mentally. The comparative absence of snow facilitated the climb up to the Cravate and to the Pic Tyndall. Here we halted for breakfast.

'To do one's job well and to eat with appetite—these are two pleasures, two joys. There is a close resemblance between a full stomach and a satisfied conscience. The azure of the sky, the infinite delicacy of its tones towards the horizon, the complete peace which prevailed, dispersed all uneasy doubt. We were delighted to feel that we had made such good progress and that we were almost certainly sure to reach the long-desired summit.

'At 9.30 we resumed our march along the shoulder. The crest was covered with snow and resembled a knife blade. Here we encountered the only serious difficulties on the climb. In less than an hour, Carrel's practical wisdom had succeeded in defeating all obstacles. At 2 p.m., fifteen hours after leaving Breuil, our party reached the summit of the Matterhorn. The view was magnificent. We revelled in its inconceivable majesty without attempting to analyse each detail. Our emotion, which was almost sacred, cannot be described.

'Encouraged by this success, I wanted to try something more, the descent to Zermatt. We were harassed by the fear that our descent towards the Swiss hut might be blocked by impossible obstacles. It was two o'clock, and only four and a half hours remained for the descent. We followed without difficulty the ridge which links the Italian with the Swiss summit in order to examine more easily the slopes which we hoped to descend. When we arrived at the cairn on the Swiss summit, the descent appeared practicable, and we immediately started downwards. Soon the sun disappeared from our eyes. The great mass of the Matterhorn projected its shadow on the Gorner Glacier and lengthened gradually towards the old Weissthor. Very magnificent was this cobalt shadow spread against the background of glacier radiant with light.

'The rocks were deep in powder snow, so that on the more difficult passages our hands, covered with thick gloves, dug deep into the snow and found no hold. Our boots froze hard in the cold snow, snowballs attached themselves to the soles, augmenting the chances of a slip. We soon reached the chains, and although they were covered with snow their assistance was invaluable . . .

'At 7.30 p.m. we arrived at last at the old hut just as the stars began to sparkle in the immensity of the heavens, while the fading twilight reflected by the snows of Monte Rosa still feebly lit our path.

'Half-an-hour's work with the ice axes was necessary to open the doors of our refuge, and even when we had broken in, we had to devote more than an hour to clearing the refuge of fresh and powdery snow that had insinuated itself through the cracks in the door and the roof. At last we sat down in that corner of the hut which was least exposed to draught. We huddled together for warmth and passed the night without sleeping, stamping our feet to prevent them freezing. Intoxicated by our success, we recalled with pride the difficulties that we had met and overcome, and the dangers which we had faced and evaded. One story followed another, and the night passed quickly. At six o'clock we resumed our descent to Zermatt, where we arrived at two o'clock in the afternoon.'

CHAPTER XVII

Mummery and the Zmutt Ridge

Alfred Frederick Mummery (1856-95) was even more representative of his period than Whymper of what is known as the Golden Age of mountaineering. Whymper created no school and is not identified with any startling innovations. Mummery, on the other hand, was a born rebel, and not only against Alpine orthodoxy, for his revolutionary economic theories, though they attracted little attention at the time, have since been widely accepted.

'As a climber', writes Geoffrey Young, 'he was unsurpassed in his day: a supreme ice man — the equal at least, as Norman Collie wrote to me last year, of the best professionals — a first rate rock climber, of the new order of rock climbing, and, moreover, gifted with a dynamic personality, at once detached, original and electrifying, which rose above the challenge of difficulty or danger with serene humour. It was this personal magnetism which led his expert parties to trust unquestioningly to his tactical leadership upon any ascent or in any crisis.'

Mummery's influence was immense and endures to this day, as is clear from the many tributes paid to him in a modern classic, *Les Alpinistes Célèbres*, published in 1956, as for instance Mlle. Micheline Morin's tribute: 'The personality of Mummery dominates this period of Alpine history. He was an innovator, and the head of a school. He attracted a group of enthusiastic climbers.' Or Alain de Chatellus' verdict in the same volume: 'Mummery's book made many disciples in the succeeding generations, more perhaps on the Continent than in his own country. The great individualists who formed the Alpine élite up to 1930 all more or less derive from him.'

Mummery paid his first visit to the Alps in 1871 and walked up to the summit of the easy Théodule Pass.

He climbed Monte Rosa in 1873 when he was seventeen, and the Matterhorn in the following year. His first famous climb was the ascent of the Zmutt ridge of the Matterhorn in 1879 when he was twenty-three years of age. On the descent from the Tiefenmattenjoch, Mummery 'gazed long and earnestly at the great Zmutt ridge' and came to the conclusion that it 'offered an obtrusively easy route to a height of about 13,000 feet, and on the final ridge, from about 14,000 feet to the summit, the climber had little to fear. Serious difficulty was limited to the short section of the route by which these two highways would have to be connected'.

His first objective on reaching Zermatt was to find a reliable guide. He was delighted to discover that Alexander Burgener might be free in a few days. Burgener, on being interviewed, expressed the opinion that 'to go on such an expedition with a Herr of whom he knew nothing would be a *"verfluchte Dummheit"* '. Mummery was impressed by Burgener's candour which seemed to him 'not merely indicative of a wise distrust of an untried climber, but also of a determination to drive home the attack, when once begun, to the utmost limits of possibility'.[1]

After four days' climbing in the course of which Mummery and Burgener achieved 'a new and remarkably difficult route on the Fletschhorn', Burgener had no further doubts, but felt they had earned a day's rest. Towards evening they heard that William Penhall had started for a bivouac and intended to assault the Zmutt ridge the next day. They had little doubt that he would succeed, and were proportionately elated when a fierce hurricane next day rendered victory impossible. They decided to spend the day at the Stockje and hoped that the weather would improve. On arriving at the Stockje, his guides, Alexander Burgener and Augustin Gentinetta, however, came to the conclusion that the weather was hopeless. Mummery was 'too young and eager' to contemplate returning and continued to forecast good weather in spite of the obvious contempt with which Gentinetta treated his predictions. Gentinetta was sent back to

[1] This and the other quotations in this chapter are from *My Climbs in the Alps and Caucasus*, Chapter I.

[Photo: Swissair]

8. The North Face of the Matterhorn, with (left) the East Face

[Photo: Swissair

19. The Breuil face of the Matterhorn. To the right, the Furggen
ridge; to the left, the Zmutt ridge

[Photo: Swissair]

20. The East Face; to the left, the Furggen ridge, to the right, the Hörnli ridge

21. A. F. Mummery

Zermatt for more supplies, and with instructions to return with the best man he could find to carry them.

Mummery retired to a quiet nook and tried to drown his anxieties in sleep.

'Late in the afternoon Burgener awoke me with a great thump and bid me look at the weather. My first impression was that he had come to upbraid me as an imposter, and hold up my prophesies to scorn and derision. His jubilant air and a look of thinness about the lingering clouds, however, negatived these painful thoughts and I found that the thump was intended to convey devout appreciation of my astounding wisdom!'

The reputation which Mummery thereby established as weather prophet was never shaken and Burgener continued to regard him 'as of transcendent merit in this branch of the climber's craft'.

About eight o'clock Gentinetta returned, bringing with him Johann Petrus. 'No bolder climber or more resolute man has ever delighted the heart of an eager Herr'. After an intensely cold night they left next morning at 4.15 a.m. At 5.20 a.m. they reached the foot of the Zmutt ridge, and climbed rapidly to the rock teeth which terminate the ridge and which, when seen from Zermatt, stand out so conspicuously against the sky. Higher up where the ridge merges into the great west face they turned to the right and followed the broken west face until it was possible to traverse back on to the Zmutt ridge which was then followed to the summit. The trickiest part of the climb was the traverse after they had left the third of the three teeth with which the snow ridge ends.

'For some reason', writes Mummery, 'probably to get a decent excuse for unroping Gentinetta and saving him from the risk of the "unknown quantity", Burgener told us to pay him out till he should be "*ganz fest*". We paid out a hundred feet of rope, and as there was no immediate prospect of his being "*ganz fest*", and as in the event of a slip it was tolerably certain that it would make no difference whether he were or no, I cautiously followed his track; Gentinetta bringing up the rear, free from the dangerous entanglement of the rope . . . On more than one occasion

I have found Burgener attempting to save others from risks which he himself was running by various more or less transparent devices. To those who know him it is needless to add that he never allows others to run risks from which he himself is exempt.'

They soon reached good firm rock which, though steep, offered 'good hold and plenty of it', the only casualty being a fatal accident to Burgener's pipe which had been jerked out of his coat pocket when the coat had been caught by a splinter of rock. At 1.45 p.m. Mummery and his guides reached the summit, and the first great climb of his brilliant career was safely accomplished.

But Mummery's was not the only party that day on the Zmutt face of the Matterhorn. Penhall's first attempt had, as we have seen, been ruined by a storm, and on his descent from his bivouac to Zermatt, Penhall met Mummery on his way to the Stockje. Penhall's guides were as pessimistic as Burgener and Gentinetta about the weather and they continued their descent to Zermatt. Shortly after arriving in Zermatt, Penhall's guide, L. Zurbrucken consulted the parish priest who assured him that the weather was mending. His predictions were received with less scepticism than those of Mummery. Penhall's guides accordingly busied themselves collecting provisions, and at 10 p.m. they left Zermatt for the foot of the great Zmutt face. Penhall's route was more direct than Mummery's and indeed he might have claimed to have made the first direct ascent of the Zmutt face, Mummery's route being a combination of Zmutt ridge and Zmutt face. Actually the Penhall route and Mummery route met about 600 feet below the actual summit. Penhall reached the summit a little over an hour later than Mummery, at 3 p.m. to be precise. Penhall considered that Mummery's route, though easier, was also more dangerous because of the greater risk of falling stones. His own route he considered consistently difficult but much safer.

Three days later J. Baumann with the guides Johan Petrus of Switzerland and Emile Rey of Italy repeated Mummery's route in an exceptionally fast time, arriving at the summit at 8.46 a.m.

Within three days three amateurs and six guides had climbed

the Zmutt face of the Matterhorn. Of these nine experts, seven were to die on mountains: Imseng in 1881 on Monte Rosa; Petrus in 1882 on the Aiguille Blanche de Pétéret; Penhall in 1882 in an avalanche on the Wetterhorn; Baumann climbing in Africa; Emile Rey in 1895 on the Dent du Géant; Mummery in the Himalaya in 1895 and Alexander Burgener in an ice avalanche below the Bergli Hut in 1910.

In the following year, 1880, Mummery made the first crossing of the Col du Lion and the first ascent of the Aiguille du Charmoz, and in 1881 he made the first ascent of the Grépon which set a new standard of rock climbing, and which was perhaps his most outstanding climb. He was among the first British to attempt really difficult climbs without guides. On July 25, 1893, Mummery, J. N. Collie, G. Hastings and W. C. Slingsby were the first British to make a *guideless* ascent of an important virgin peak. The Dent du Requin was the peak in question. In 1888 Mummery visited the Caucasus, and with a Meiringen guide, Heinrich Zurflüh, made the first ascent of Dychtau (17,054 feet). In 1895 Mummery disappeared in an attempt on Nanga Parbat, probably swept to destruction by an ice-avalanche.

Mummery, as I have said, was from the first in revolt against Alpine orthodoxy as expounded, for instance, in the Badminton volume on Mountaineering at which he frequently poked fun, and this perhaps was one reason why he was blackballed at his first attempt to be elected to the Alpine Club. Prior to 1938, the names of candidates whose mountaineering qualifications had been approved by the committee were submitted to a secret ballot of all members present at one of the monthly meetings of the club, one blackball in ten excluding. In practice this meant that a clique of a dozen members could keep anybody out of the club.[1] Mummery, who was blackballed at his first attempt, is described in the Alpine Club Register as 'Partner with his brother in a tanning business at Dover and Canterbury'. It was believed by some members that Mummery had a retail shop at Dover, and that prejudice against the retail trade may have been a factor, but C. H. Pasteur who was in a good position to know, always

---

[1] For fuller details of many notorious cases of candidates being blackballed see *A Century of Mountaineering*, pp. 98-102.

maintained that the only cause of the blackballing was jealousy on the part of Sir Edward Davidson.

Davidson always climbed with two first-class guides, and had a somewhat undistinguished career as a mountaineer. He was said to 'have dined and wined himself into the Presidency of the Alpine Club'. Count Aldo Bonacossa, an honorary member of the Alpine Club, told me an amusing story about an encounter with Davidson in the Schönbühl hut. A Genevese student put his rucksack on a bunk which Davidson had intended to claim. Davidson pointed to the offending rucksack with a look of deep disgust, turned to his guide, Franz Lochmatter, and said, 'Ôtezle'. The Genevese student, a member of the Swiss Alpine Club which built the hut, expostulated angrily. My friend Aldo Bonacossa, a natural diplomat of genius, drew him aside. 'You must not take him too seriously, he is a character. One must not get too cross with characters.' Meanwhile Lochmatter turned beseeching eyes on Bonacossa, eyes which in effect said 'Do help. We can do *nothing* with Herr Davidson.' The student very decently gave in and some little time later Bonacossa met Lochmatter who expressed his heartfelt gratitude for his timely intervention.

Mummery was not only an exceptionally brilliant climber, he was also the author of one of the best beloved of Alpine classics, *My Climbs in the Alps and Caucasus.* I was six years old when I read my first adult book, *Scrambles amongst the Alps,* and seven when I read Mummery's classic which had just been published in 1895. My father had bought a copy which I eventually annexed. It is therefore a little difficult for me dispassionately to judge a book which had such a profound influence on me when I first read it seventy years ago, and which I still admire, even though I am now conscious of certain defects such as the polysyllabic facetiousness of referring to the Devil as His Satanic Majesty or arch allusions to swearing as, for instance:

'It is distinctly unpleasant when a companion, whom you think is enjoying himself, suddenly informs you that he is doubtful of his power to stand in the steps. . . . At such times nothing but the fact that one has been brought up surrounded by the best religious influences, prevents the ejaculation of the strongest and most soul-satisfying expletives known to the English tongue.'

But in spite of dated mannerisms, time has not eroded the intense vitality of the great passages which convey, as only the greatest of Alpine classics convey, the joy of mountain battle.

For Mummery, however, the mountains were far more than a mere arena for athletic achievement. His book opens with a passage which is perhaps the noblest overture in Alpine literature.

'At the age of fifteen the crags of the Via Mala and the snows of the Théodule roused a passion within me that has grown with years, and has to no small extent moulded my life and thought. It has led me into regions of such fairy beauty that the fabled wonders of Zanadu seem commonplace beside them; it has brought me friends who may be relied on in fair weather and in foul; and it has stored my mind with memories that are treasures, corruptible neither by moth nor rust, sickness nor old age. My boyish delight in the great white peaks towering above the gloom of pines is still awakened when the lumbering diligence rolls through the gorge of the Diosaz or when the Matterhorn rises from out the foliage of the Val Tournanche. I remember, as if it were yesterday, my first sight of the great mountain. It was shining in all the calm majesty of a September moon, and, in the stillness of an autumn night, it seemed the very embodiment of mystery and a fitting dwelling-place for the spirits with which old legends people its stone-swept slopes.'

In all the literature which the Matterhorn has inspired there are few more eloquent and more moving passages than this.

NOTES

The first guideless ascent of the Zmutt was achieved by Charles Gos and a young Dutchman, Jean Kappeyne, both students at Geneva. As they reached the summit they met Geoffrey Young and Rudolf Lochmatter on his first climb after losing a hand in an accident. According to Gos, Young and Lochmatter had climbed unroped! This fortunate encounter was the beginning of a long friendship.

Charles Gos, the son of a famous Alpine painter, Albert Gos, is the author of that very interesting book, *Le Cervin*, an anthology, with informed comments, of the famous Matterhorn climbs.

The Zmutt 'Diretissima'. This, the most direct route up the Zmutt face to the summit, was achieved on August 13, 1962, by Giovanni Ottin and Renato Daguin.

CHAPTER XVIII

Guido Rey and the Furggen Ridge

The classic Matterhorn climbs are, with one exception, closely linked in our memory with the names of those who made the first ascents—the Matterhorn itself with Whymper, the Italian ridge with Jean Antoine Carrel, the Zmutt ridge with Mummery, and the north face with the brothers Schmid. The one exception is the Furggen ridge which seems far less closely associated with Mario Piacenza, who was the first to climb it, then with Guido Rey who failed within a few rope-lengths of the summit. We remember Rey's near-success because it is described in an Alpine classic, *Il Monte Cervino*, a book which we treasure not only as a moving and authentic expression of mountain love but also because of its historical value, for Rey was on terms of intimate friendship with the Italian pioneers, Quintino Sella, Felice Giordano and J. A. Carrel. All those who have written about the early Italian attempts on the Matterhorn, and Carrel's first ascent of the Italian ridge, are indebted, as is the present writer, to Rey's book.

Guido Rey, who was born at Turin in 1861 and died in 1935, was French on his mother's side, for his mother was the daughter of the Marquis de Renancourt (Besançon). He was a nephew of Quintino Sella, founder of the Italian Alpine Club, who had married the sister of Rey's father. Guido Rey received a classical education before being associated with his father's interests in wool and cloth. He travelled widely as a representative of his father's business, spent long periods abroad, and mastered many languages.[1] His tastes were artistic, and he was on terms of

[1] I should like to record my indebtedness to Armando Biancardi's charming sketch of Guido Rey which will be found on pages 243 and 244 of Alfonso Bernardi's excellent anthology, *Il Gran Cervino*.

intimate friendship with many contemporary artists. His approach to Alpine literature was the approach of an artist whose medium is the written word. His instinctive sympathy with any Alpine writer who attempted not merely to record mountain adventure but also to interpret his response to the majesty and mystery of mountain beauty, found very moving expression in a letter which gave great delight to a young man, the present writer, whose book, *The Mountains of Youth*, had found favour with Rey.

His own mountain creed was expressed in words which are difficult to translate, for in English they read a shade too rhetorically. *Io credetti e credo la lotta coll'Alpi utile como il lavoro, nobile come un'arte, bella come una fede.* 'I believed and believe the struggle against the mountains to be of use as work, to be noble as an art, and to be beautiful as a faith.' I am quoting from the preface to *Alpinismo Acrobatico*.

Rey climbed in most of the great Alpine ranges. He made the first Italian ascent of the Meije, and climbed peaks like the Grépon and the Dru when they were still considered very difficult. He had a special affection for the Dolomites, and among his many Dolomite ascents may be mentioned the south face of the Marmolata. He was a pioneer of guideless climbing in Italy.

In the first world war he volunteered for active service, but volunteers of his age, sixty-one, were not accepted. He placed his car at the disposal of a voluntary ambulance unit, and was frequently in the battle zone. A motoring accident near the front put an end to his mountaineering. Rey never married. He died at the age of seventy-four in 1935.

Rey's *Il Monte Cervino* was admirably translated by J. E. C. Eaton. A revised edition with two additional chapters by a distinguished British mountaineer, R. L. G. Irving, was published by Basil Blackwell in 1946. 'If we can divest ourselves', writes Mr Irving, 'of our rigid prejudice against the free expression of strong emotion—a prejudice that is said to have originated in imitation of the Duke of Wellington—and if we can understand Rey's passionate feeling for the mountain, the thrill that went through him as his fingers grasped its virgin rocks and halted for a moment on a ledge first trodden by Italian feet, we may be able to see the matter with his eyes. More than any other incident in his book it justifies what his great friend de Amicis wrote in the preface: "In this feeling for the mountain Guido Rey lays his whole soul bare". Moreover, it is an Italian not a British soul.'

It is indeed an Italian soul, and some of the passages which are most charged with emotion provoke no particular comment in Italian but read a little strangely in the English translation, as for instance the passage describing his return from his failure, within sight of success, on the Furggen ridge. Outside his hotel Rey met a friend of his, a member of the Alpine Club. Here is Rey's record of that meeting in the original Italian:

' "*Ebbene?*" *mi chiese.*

'*Questa semplice domanda mi diede un colpo terribile; sentii la gola che mi serrava, un singhiozzo ne saliva, e, se avessi risposto, avrei pianto.*

'*Non piansi. I preguidizi umani negano a chi vuol sembrare forte questa nobilissima espressione dell'animo. L'alpinista vuol essere di sasso come la sua montagna, il mio pianto avrebbe fatto ridere; entrai nell'albergo, fra gli uomini, con la maschera dell'indifferenza.*'

In this passage an Italian soul, to quote Mr Irving, finds characteristic expression in the Italian language. Here is Mr Eaton's translation:

' "Well?" he said.

'His simple question affected me terribly; my throat contracted, a sob arose in it, and if I had answered I should have wept. But I did not weep, for human prejudices deny this noble expression of feeling to those who wish to appear strong. The climber wishes to be thought as hard as the mountain he climbs, and if I had wept I should have made others laugh. I entered the hotel and mingled with its denizens, wearing the mask of indifference.'

An Englishman who thought it worth while to record the fact that it had not been easy to control his emotions would express himself very differently, and in the English translation one often unconsciously judges Rey by English standards, and

(a)

(b)

2

(a) Vittorio Sella at
twenty-five years

(b) Guido Rey in 1904

[Photo: Paola Sella]

[Photo: Mrs Winthrop Young]

23. Geoffrey Winthrop Young

this, as that distinguished Wykamist, Mr R. L. G. Irving, reminds us, is unreasonable.

In 1893 Rey made three unsuccessful attempts on the Furggen ridge, and did not return to the attack until 1899. His dramatic story of his near-success is invaluable as a record of what he *felt* but is not quite so satisfactory as a record of what Clough calls 'The merest "it was".' The actual date of the climb, August 24-26, 1899, for instance, is not recorded.

Rey engaged three guides, Antoine, Aimé and Daniel Maquignaz, of whom Antoine and Aimé were to accompany Rey up the Furggen ridge while Daniel and two men whom Rey does not name climbed the Matterhorn by the ordinary Swiss route, taking with them 200 metres of rope. From the summit Daniel Maquignaz and his companions were to descend the Furggen ridge to a point as close as possible to the highest point reached by Rey and his guides in their ascent of the Furggen ridge. The plan was to lower the 200-metre rope, by the help of which Rey and his guides would then complete the ascent. If this plan had succeeded, purists would certainly have argued that no mountaineer can claim to have climbed a ridge if he is helped up the more difficult pitches by a rope lowered from above.

After a five hours' night march, Rey and his guides reached the Breuiljoch with the first light of dawn. The Furggen ridge up to the Furggen shoulder, *circa* 14,000 feet, is a straight-forward climb, and it is only above the Furggen shoulder that the real difficulties begin. Mummery had reached this shoulder in 1880 but considered that the last section was unclimbable. He had accordingly traversed across the east face to the Swiss shoulder, a dangerous traverse exposed to constant bombardment by falling stones, and completed the ascent by the normal Swiss route.

Rey looked up at the appalling cliff above him, and could detect no practicable route, but his guides spoke of a hidden chimney 120 feet above, which they believed to be the clue to the ascent. Meanwhile they waited, for it was useless to proceed until Daniel and his companions had completed the ascent and descended as far as possible on the Furggen ridge. After an hour and a half's wait they heard a faint shout from above, and before long Aimé and Antoine were exchanging shouts with Daniel.

H

'At last,' writes Rey, 'not far above my head I could see the end of a rope, descending silently, as if it were a small snake creeping insidiously towards me with peculiar halts, leaps and writhings. It seemed alive; then it stopped a few metres from me. It was the thread which was to lead us out of the Minataur's cave.'

With the indispensable assistance of this rope, let down from above, Rey and his guides proceeded to climb a chimney with few holds, and those of little value since the strata sloped downwards. The slight assistance which the sides of the chimney afforded ended when they emerged from the chimney on to the open cliff. The vertical route they were to follow was indicated by the position of the great rope. Rey swung from side to side as he hoisted himself upwards by struggles and contortions, his feet often kicking uncertainly into space.

The party spent four hours climbing 300 vertical feet from the shoulder, and arrived at a point a little over a hundred yards in distance from the summit. One of the sacks which contained Rey's Kodak was hoisted up to the summit. 'Happy little Kodak,' mused Rey, 'you have conquered the Furggen ridge.'

Antoine seized the rope which was hanging inside the curve of the cliff, climbed three or four rope lengths by pulling on the rope and scraping the rock with his feet. He lost his footing and came down again. Rey's account of what followed is not very clear, and after reading it more than once both in the original Italian and in Mr J. E. C. Eaton's excellent translation, I still cannot understand why only one rope was used on the final section. If a fixed rope had been left in position, and if a second rope had been lowered to Antoine and attached to his body, Antoine could have hoisted himself up the fixed rope vigorously assisted by Daniel and other men tugging on the rope round his body. In this case surely the obstacle must have been overcome. Rey makes no attempt to explain why this obvious procedure was not adopted.

'I asked Daniel', writes Rey, 'to throw him down a knotted rope, and forthwith the whole long rope was pulled up by Daniel, and in the upper laboratory he and his men employed themselves busily in tying two ropes together in such a way as to form a single knotted rope.' This they eventually lowered, and this single knotted rope appears to have been the only rope used. Antoine fastened it as best as he could in a crack in the rocks, and then began to climb it. On his success depended the issue between victory and defeat.

The rope, though fixed at the bottom, was pulled out of place by his weight. He began to swing to and fro. He was, we are told, paralyzed by 'the uncertain oscillation of the rope'. He held himself for a few moments, writes Rey, 'by one of the knots', tried to draw his body near to the rock, and shouted to those above . . . and then, slowly lowered himself, reached the base of the final obstacle, relinquished the rope and came towards Rey. Rey asked him if all hope were gone. He answered that nothing could be done. 'If faudrait une echelle.' Yes, they needed a ladder, and without it the ten yards which had separated Antoine from those above had proved decisive. They were defeated.

Two days later they returned to the attack. They climbed the Italian ridge, carrying with them two long rope-ladders. During a breakfast halt on the shoulder, one of them exclaimed, '*Diable! Le Mont Blanc a mis son chapeau.*' Bad news, for a cloud-cap on Mont Blanc has a tendency to widen its brim until many other mountains are covered.

Before nine they were on the summit of the Matterhorn, and after a short pause started down the Furggen ridge, watching with growing anxiety the approach of a storm. At eleven they reached the point which Daniel's party had reached on the day of their failure. The Théodule was by now clouded, and the first peels of thunder awakened echoes in the Matterhorn cliffs.

With the aid of the rope ladders Rey descended to the point which he had reached on his previous attempt, and reascended on the rope ladder 'which swayed gaily, tossed to and fro in the wind like a light piece of ribbon'. Rey rejoined the guides. 'The ceremony was over.'

'Next day,' writes Rey, 'calm in mind and rested in my body I reviewed all that had occurred and arrived at a clear conception of what had happened. I had been the first to climb, either up or down, every point on the Furggen ridge, and had, in a manner of speaking, taken possession of it. And yet I was not satisfied.

I felt that I had taken by surprise the ancient Matterhorn and such warfare was not honourable. It was the conquered rather than the conqueror who would have won the approval of a Cato among mountaineers'—*sed victa Catoni*—'such was my respect for my great foe that I knew that I should have conquered him face to face on the first day.

'No! The Matterhorn had once again defeated me, not I the Matterhorn.'

Rey was amused by a comment in a Genevese paper: '*Le clubiste italien qui s'est fait hisser au Cervin par l'arête surplombante de Furggen mériterait une amende. C'est un fou dangereux.*' And Rey adds, 'On my honour I have never discovered this before, but no man is a judge of himself'.

'It is difficult to imagine', writes Mr Irving, 'any English climber (whether north or south of the Border) going through this last performance of Rey's. Failure to climb an impossibly difficult rock pitch cannot be changed into success by being let down over it from above. As exploration in view of a future ascent the thing has been done on Welsh rocks and elsewhere, and as a rule, a discreet silence has been maintained about it till the ascent has followed. Rey never made another attempt. Perhaps he recognized that the place was not climbable by any methods he cared to employ.'

I agree, of course, with Mr Irving that Rey cannot be considered to have made the first ascent of the Furggen ridge, and indeed Rey himself made no such claim, but I am startled by Mr. Irving's apparent belief that 'Mummery had seriously invalidated any future claims to conquest of the Furggen ridge by an ascent in 1880'. Mummery in his 1880 attempt stopped at the very point where the real difficulties began, and, as we have seen, traversed across to the Swiss shoulder and completed the ascent from there.

'At that time', writes Mr Irving, 'no casuist thought of disputing a claim to the ascent of a great mountain by one of its main ridges because some apparently insurmountable step had been turned by a traverse on one side or the other.'

One does not need to follow every yard of a ridge to substantiate a claim to have climbed it, but such deviations must be of minor importance. My own view is that Mario Piacenza deserves the credit for making the first ascent of the Furggen ridge on September 4, 1909. Mario Piacenza with three Valtournanche guides, Joseph Pelissier, Joseph Carrel and J. Gaspard, left the Hörnli hut in the early hours, waited for the dawn on the Breuiljoch, and climbed rapidly to the Furggen shoulder. Here they left the main ridge for a traverse on the south face which brought them to a steep rockwall which they climbed by a human ladder, Piacenza on Gaspard's shoulder and Gaspard on Carrel's. The difficulties continued to be extreme, and another human ladder was necessary before they finally regained the Furggen ridge just above the overhang which had stopped Guido Rey.

A year later Pelissier died in Piacenza's arms after an ascent of Elbruz.

No more direct ascent of the Furggen ridge was possible without either the help of a rope lowered from above, as in the case of Rey's ascent, or of hammering a ladder of pitons into the cliff —the modern method. The first *direct* ascent of the Furggen ridge was finally achieved thirty-one years later by Luigi Carrel, son of the Joseph Carrel who led Piacenza on the first ascent of the Furggen ridge.

On September 22, 1942, Alfredo Perino, an engineer, with the guides Luigi Carrel ('Carrelino') and Giacomo Chiara, reached at 10.40 the point where the real difficulties begin. At 11 a.m. Carrel, linked to his companions by two fifty-metre ropes, started up the cliff. Eight hours were spent on the ascent of a little over 300 vertical feet. Two hours were spent on one particular pitch only a few metres in height. Twice it was necessary for Carrel to stand on Chiara's shoulders. The nervous strain was not mitigated, as in the case of Rey's party, by the use of a long rope lowered by friends near the summit. The climb would have been absolutely impossible without the aid of the forty-three *pitons* which Carrel hammered into the cliff. Such a climb is an extreme test not only of nerve but of physical endurance. At 7.30 p.m. the summit was reached, and the problem of the first direct ascent of the Furggen ridge had been solved.

Finally on March 20, 1953, Roberto Bignani and Walter Bonatti, after a bivouac below the summit with a temperature of minus 25 degrees centigrade, completed the first ascent of the Furggen ridge in winter by the most direct route.

CHAPTER XIX

The Matterhorn with a Difference

In the opening years of the twentieth century no mountaineer had a finer record of first ascents in the Alps than Geoffrey Winthrop Young, among them a new route up the Weisshorn from Zinal, the Younggrat on the Zermatt Breithorn, the south face of the Täschhorn, the first direct ascent of the Mer de Glace face to the actual summit of the Grépon, the Jorasses from the Col des Grandes Jorasses and—his last climb before the first world war in which he was to lose a leg—the grim Red Teeth ridge of the Gspaltenhorn.

No ridge or face of the Matterhorn was first explored by Geoffrey Young, but none the less Young has an honoured place in the story of the mountain, for he was the first and so far the only mountaineer to have climbed the Matterhorn after losing a leg.

In a book which professes, as the reader will have deduced from the introduction, not only to record climbs but also to evoke the personalities of the climbers whose names are associated with the mountain, it would be inconsistent merely to summarize the chapter of *Mountains with a Difference* in which Geoffrey Young describes his one-legged climbs.

My friendship with Young began when I reviewed his first book of poems, *Wind and Hill*, for *The Isis*, the Oxford undergraduates' weekly of which I was then the editor. But for Young's encouragement I might never have produced *Oxford Mountaineering Essays*. To the end of his life he continued to exercise a great influence on the Oxford and Cambridge Mountaineering Clubs.

Shortly before the first world war I persuaded Methuens that Young should be invited to edit an up-to-date study of mountaineering technique to replace the out-of-date volume on Mountaineering in the Badminton Library. *Mountain Craft* was the result. *On High Hills*, the story of his greatest climbs, was published in 1927, and *Mountains with a Difference* in which he describes his one-legged ascents, in 1951.

Geoffrey Winthrop Young was the son of Sir George Young, Bart., an Alpine pioneer who took part in the first ascent of the Jungfrau from the Wengernalp. In the course of a guideless descent of Mont Blanc, Sir George's brother was killed. Sir George never climbed again. He was, I believe, proud of Geoffrey's climbs, but he never discussed them with me though I saw him often at a time when he was my landlord and I lived very near his home, Formosa, at Cookham. Indeed the only time he mentioned mountaineering to me was when I had just returned from a search party in the Pyrenees which was led by Geoffrey and which ended when we found the body of one of the most brilliant climbers of my generation, Hugh Pope. Sir George asked me one or two questions and then sighed deeply.

During the first world war Geoffrey Young helped to organize the Friends' Ambulance Unit which operated in and near Ypres. The Friends' Ambulance Unit had a deservedly high reputation for the care which they took to spare the wounded unnecessary pain. Of Geoffrey's sensitive sympathy I can speak from personal experience. Any chance that I might have had of tackling serious climbs with Geoffrey was ruined by a crippling smash in the mountains which removed two inches from my right leg, but at the beginning of one of his best seasons Geoffrey and I climbed the Mönch together, in his case a training walk. On our descent we found the Ewig Schneefeld particularly tiresome, and in his book *On High Hills* Young makes a passing reference to the snow 'with a crust on it that twisted each stumbling leg knee deep, and then clung to it like a trap with sharp dragging edges', all the more unpleasant because I still had an open wound in my shin. Geoffrey made no comment on the cause of my slow pace, but I was conscious of his sympathy which only became explicit later in his written allusion to that exhausting experience.

Young wrote few passages which moved me more than the chapter in his book *The Grace of Forgetting* in which he describes the splendid work of the Friends' Ambulance Unit at Ypres, which was under constant bombardment, and his co-operation with 'the heroine Soeur Marguerite' and with the Curé Del'Aere, 'the bravest man I ever knew'.

When Italy came into the war, 'we were asked', writes Young, 'to make some gesture that should reassure them politically. George Trevelyan, the friend of Italy and the historian of Garibaldi, became our commandant, and organized a unit and a committee and finance of our own, to work on the Italian front. Philip Noel Baker, who had led the first Friends' unit, also joined us.'

As a result of severe wounds incurred in the attack on Monte San Gabriele, Young's right leg had to be amputated, but he was determined to continue climbing. He invented a special mechanical peg which could be lengthened and shortened at will, and into which he introduced a spring to reduce jar. 'Mallory was resolved, as he wrote to me from the French front on the first news of my injury, that I was to return to mountaineering and "make something splendid out of it".' As indeed he did.

His return to the mountains began on Welsh cliffs, the gashed crag on Tryfan being the first of many one-legged rock climbs. He even led one rock climb.

'It was with that first-rate climber of the great Cambridge generation, Ivan Waller. Two ascents of the Tryfan Milestone buttress were behind us. It was an evening when waves of golden light were flooding warmly up the Nant Francon, and the increasing difficulties of the climbs had released in me a "second confidence" such as I had not felt since the war. With Ivan insisting, I led the so-called super-direct climb with a contented certainty.'

In 1927 he returned to the Alps. With Claude Elliott as a sympathetic and ever watchful friend, and with the guides Franz Lochmatter and Hans Brantschen, he led off with one of the longest of Alpine climbs, Monte Rosa. Sir Claude tells me that towards the end of the descent Young was so exhausted that his mind was affected, and he started talking to Donald Robertson, an old climbing friend who had been killed rock-climbing. Young admitted later that he should have begun in a region of smaller mountains, and then follows a passage which will be read with particular interest by those who have continued to climb after a crippling smash.

'On the other hand, if I had not been so unforeseeing, I should never have attempted Alpine ascents at all. If I had sat down beforehand and reckoned up the measure of the new limitations, of my slow pace and insecure movement, as against the length and difficulties I must now find upon every order of greater ascent, I should never have had the audacity to venture deliberately upon anything but the mildest type of home climbing. Fatigue and nervous discouragement in any case began to register so very early in the effort of any mountain day, that if I was to achieve anything at all, I very soon found that my only course was to disregard alike both future probabilities and present sensations, and in fact reasonableness altogether, and go blindly for the chance that offered—in hope.'

His first Alpine one-legged climb was in 1927, his last, the Zinal Rothorn, in 1935. To have made a single one-legged ascent of an Alpine peak would have been a great achievement, but to continue for more than one season was fantastic, particularly as he was then in his middle fifties. He climbed the following peaks: Monte Rosa, Wellenkuppe, Weisshorn to the foot of the final dome where dangerous snow forced a retreat, Cinque Torre, Requin, Grépon and Matterhorn. And it is with his Matterhorn ascent that I am primarily concerned in this chapter.

His leading guide was Hans Brantschen, his second guide he mercifully does not name—'I have forgotten his name happily and shall call him Thomas'. Young took a mule up to the Belvedere and started for the Matterhorn at 10 p.m. by the light of a low moon. The last steep slabs up which run fixed ropes proved to be

'strenuous acrobatics; sometimes the peg caught in the fixed chains and in the like man-made chuck-me-downs. But I found the arm-pulls warming. The angle eased off, curving up on to the summit gable. There came a happy certainty, of wonder and fulfilment, and I struggled up the final pent of snow and slab, and saw just above me the transparent fins and fans of wind-ice erect upon the narrow rock crest. I put on the pace with the shortened peg—no need now to save energy—gripped Hans by his rucksack loop, and limped on to the summit. It was seven-thirty, and we had been climbing for nine and a half hours; which was only about three times as long as I should formerly have allowed, and not the five times longer of my snow ascents. And it was my eighth ascent, with three frustrated attempts.'

They were nearly killed while descending a steep pitch of gritty rock below the shoulder, the Moseley-platte, so called because an American climber, Dr. W. O. Moseley of Boston, fell to his death at this point. 'Thomas' was the last man down. And then Thomas fell.

'My ear was startled by an irregular sound—sounds proper to climbing the ear accepts unnoticing. I turned to glance up; and a big figure came hurtling backwards over the vertical cliff above me. It crashed on to the sloping gutter beside me and bounced on into space. With his immense strength Hans, poised on the ledge beyond me, caught him in mid-air on my rope, and he banged in below us on to easier rock. I need hardly say that I could never have stopped him.

'Not one word was spoken, then or afterwards, about the fall. We all knew equally well that, under the circumstances of this ascent, such a fall, on such straightforward rock, by a guide, and by the last man, and without even a warning, was beyond all explanation, all excuse, and even beyond the pale of spoken censure. As happening among experienced climbers it was so unthinkable a crime that I felt nothing but sorrow for Thomas, who must have undermined the guiding quality he once possessed during the lax war years.'

There was no further incident on the long and exhausting descent to Zermatt where Young was warmly welcomed by Dr George Wherry, 'tall distinguished silver-haired wit and savant'.

'From my window at midnight the Matterhorn was just per-ceptible: a velvet-black column, etched here and there in its outline against the scattered stars of a serene dark-blue sky. Not the least like its own gaunt frost-rent tempestuous reality of my climbing day; but once more the superb and shrouded symbol of mountain perfection, and of all that a mountain can mean for us.'

NOTE

By an odd coincidence I was nearly killed on this same Moseley-platte by an equally inexplicable lapse. My father had left Alexander Seiler to decide whether I needed a second guide, and the second guide who was forced on me fell off the Moseley-platte and carried me with him. But my leading guide, a grandson of the older Taugwalder of the Matterhorn first ascent, though utterly unprepared for 'so unthinkable a crime', held us both as we swung round, a magnificent effort both of balance and strength. Unlike 'Thomas', my second guide was not 'beyond the pale of spoken censure', for throughout the rest of the ascent Taugwalder maintained a steady stream of invective.

CHAPTER XX

The North Face and the Brothers Schmid

Towards the end of July 1931 two brothers, Toni and Franz Schmid, mounted their bicycles at Munich and arrived at Zermatt a few days later. Three years had passed since Toni Schmid had first seen the Matterhorn. He had been fascinated by the north face, and had hardly dared to admit even to himself his ambition to solve the last great problem of the most famous of Alpine peaks. What he saw was not exactly encouraging, for the north face seemed to be subjected to a fairly constant bombardment of falling rock and ice.

Toni Schmid told the story of their climb in *La Montagne*, March 1932. Only July 28, 1931, the brothers pitched their tent on the Staffelalp, and on July 29th they explored the route which they were to follow through the séracs of the Matterhorn glacier to the base of the north wall. They rested on July 30th, and at midnight they were awakened by their alarm clock. The weather was not too promising, for there was a touch of foehn in the air and streaky clouds in the sky. They left a note of their plan in the tent, for the information of a possible search party, and reached the Hörnli hut at 2 a.m. on the morning of July 31st.

There were the usual climbing parties in the hut, climbers who would climb the Matterhorn by the east face as far as the shoulder, and then reach the summit by a few hundred feet up the north face. The hut keeper agreed to warn all climbers that the brothers would be on the north face, and to beg them to be very careful not to detach loose stones on the final northern section.

Following the route which they had already explored, the brothers reached the foot of an ice slope a thousand vertical feet in height, grooved by falling stones. The time was 3.45 a.m. and it was still dark. They rested until 4 a.m., and by then there was just enough light to attempt the ice slope. They cut no steps and trusted themselves to their ten-pointed crampons. Only climbers with perfect balance and superb nerve would dare to tackle ice at a gradient of sixty degrees without cutting a single step, an effort which was not only a supreme test of nerve but also of endurance, for the cramped position of their feet as they balanced on the crampons was exhausting and painful.

They were faced with a choice of risks. By climbing on their crampons without cutting steps, they took a chance. On the other hand, if they had cut steps they would have been exposed far longer to the far greater risk of falling stones. Toni led throughout, driving in an ice piton to give security at each rope's length.

The clue to the ascent of the north face is a long, shallow gully which starts near the top right-hand corner of the ice-slope, and slants upwards obliquely until it fades out in steep rocks about the level of the Swiss shoulder. In order to reach this gully they had to traverse not only across ice but also across rocks covered with a thin film of ice into which holds had to be chipped out with great accuracy. Across this traverse Franz led.

In the early hours of the day the gully, which they had now entered, is glazed with ice, and the brothers sometimes climbed the icy centre of the gully and sometimes the rocks at the side. As the temperature rose and the ice glaze thawed, water streamed down the gully, but the heavy snowfalls earlier in July, though they increased the difficulty of the climb, had also greatly reduced the risk from falling stones. None the less, 'stones of every size' from time to time fell uncomfortably close.

The sun was sinking when they at last reached the slabs above the gully by a difficult chimney and a short ice-wall. They were now at a height of about 13,000 feet above the sea, and some 1,500 feet below the summit. For hour after hour they had been exposed to the most exacting test of nerve, of physical strength and of sensitive balance, and the strain was beginning to tell. Their fingers were not only scratched and bleeding but also chilled by constant contact with icy rocks. They were tormented by thirst.

Shortly before they bivouaced a catastrophe was averted by the narrowest of margins. Toni was below and Franz was leading, and the rope between them was belayed round a projecting rock. Suddenly the rock on which Toni was standing broke away and crashed down the mountain side. Toni flung out his arms, and his fingers closed on a narrow rocky ledge and checked his fall, but his feet vainly sought for some support, and without such support he could neither advance nor hold on indefinitely. Franz by a supreme effort was able to drag him up a few inches until Toni's feet at last established contact with a small rocky ledge.

The shadows were lengthening on the glacier below, and the inexorable night was closing in, and they had yet to find a bivouac site. It was not until 8.30 p.m. that they found a ledge on which it was just, but only just, possible to bivouac, a minute rocky platform measuring no more than one square metre. *Pitons* were driven into the rocks, and to these *pitons* they attached themselves with a rope. Crampons and axes were tied to another *piton*. The utmost care was essential, for anything dropped vanished into the abyss below, as Hilti von Allmen's crampons were to vanish when he bivouaced during the first winter ascent of this same north face.

They contrived to extract without disaster their rubber sleeping bag and food from their rucksacks, and to still the pangs of hunger with bread, butter, cheese and dried fruit, after which they packed themselves into their sleeping sack. Before the sun sank they had been worried by gathering clouds, for their chances of survival would have been small indeed had they been caught by a violent storm while still on the north face, but the elements were merciful, and the storm which they dreaded did not break until they reached the summit next day.

They passed the night huddled together in their rubber sack, a miserable night, for there was no room to move or to change position, and they suffered tortures of cramp. They greeted the dawn with shouts of joy, but it was two hours before the sun reached them and warmed their stiff limbs, and it was 7 a.m. before they returned to the attack.

They followed a promising rock rib, and were beginning to hope that their difficulties were over, but they were soon undeceived, for the comparatively easy rib ended in smooth slabs of rock into which it was impossible even to drive a *piton*. Franz suggested a traverse to the left which would have led them on to the shoulder, on the normal Swiss route. Toni demurred because he was anxious to complete the climb on the north face proper rather than on the left ridge of the north face which the normal Swiss route follows from the shoulder upwards. His choice was confirmed by advice shouted to the brothers by Alexander Pollinger who had appeared over the shoulder while they were hestitating. He shouted to them that the traverse to the left was impossible, so Franz turned to the right, crossed a ledge of rotten snow on to slabs covered with ice just, but only just, thick enough to allow shallow steps to be cut. Would the steps hold? And what would happen if they did not? They had no time to weigh such possibilities for the weather had suddenly deteriorated, and flurries of cold mist broke on the cliffs. With the energy of desperation they hurried up a series of snow-filled cracks leading ever upwards into the mist, cracks which from time to time were interrupted by short pitches of smooth rock. The wind became a hurricane which lashed their faces with driven hail. But the tempest was too late to destroy them, for the slope had eased off and nothing could stop them now. The peals of thunder and flashes of lightning seemed, wrote Toni Schmid, 'to signify that the mountain could not reconcile itself to defeat'. The storm reached its climax as the brothers reached the summit. It was 2 p.m. on August 1, 1931.

They grounded their axes, dangerous lightning conductors in a storm, cowered beneath a rock and silently clasped hands. When Abbé Sieyès was asked to describe his life during the French Revolution he replied quite simply, 'J'ai surveçu' ('I survived'). Much the same reply might have been given by the Schmid brothers if invited to summarize their impressions of their fantastic climb.

When the storm seemed to have spent its fury, the brothers started down the ordinary route, grateful for the fixed ropes on the steeper pitches between the summit and the shoulder. 'In comparison', wrote Toni, 'with the difficulties which we had

[Photo: Hilti von Almen]

24. Paul Etter, while making the first winter ascent of the North Face

25

Tante Biner and her
letter to Whymper

Zermatt the 3. th 19

Dear Mr. Whymper!

*Your friendlye line have my
veri surprised and pleasd.
I Thank You veri much for Your
good offer I am veri glad.
All reglt. the memory of You
will never dei. I will make You
beautiful. My Salutation and
Thank to You.*

*I remain Your most
obediently Marie. Biner.*

overcome, the descent was mere play.' But the 'mere play' phase
did not last very long, for below the shoulder they had to battle
against a storm even more violent than that which had buffeted
them on the summit. Hail and snow poured down the rocks.
Their rope, coated with ice, was more of a menace than a protection. And then the Solvay hut, the haven of their hopes,
shaped itself out of the driving snow. They had survived.

They stumbled into the hut. Their fingers could only with
difficulty untie their rope. Their clothes were so frozen that
when taken off they stood up like armour. They ate the last of
their food, wrapped every blanket which they could find round
their bodies, and slept until noon next day.

It was still snowing when they looked out of the hut. They
made a poor meal from the emergency rations which are kept in
the hut for emergencies such as this, and went back to bed. Next
morning, August 3rd, the sun broke through the clouds, and at
7 a.m. the brothers left the hut. The heavy snowfall had covered
the easy rocks, and the utmost care was necessary to ensure that
their triumph was not to end, as the triumph of the first ascent
had ended, in tragedy.

Meanwhile nothing was known of their fate at Zermatt. They
had been seen near the summit on August 1st. Had they reached
the Solvay hut before night fell? Or had they been forced to
bivouac in the storm? August 2nd passed without any sign of
the missing brothers. On August 3rd when the brothers started
their descent, their friends were already moving up the mountain
to meet them, and the joyful reunion took place just after mid-
day. By this time the brothers were famished, and the provisions
which their friends had brought with them were more than
welcome. At 2 p.m. they scrambled down the last rocks leading
to the Hörnli hut where they were enthusiastically cheered by
a group of climbers. There was great joy in Zermatt when at last
they reached the village. Here they spent a few nights as Dr
Seiler's personal guests, and a dinner was organized in their
honour.

Poor Toni did not live long to enjoy his fame. A year later he
was leading a very difficult climb on the north-west face of the
Gross-Wiesbachhorn. An ice *piton* on which Toni was relying
broke away, and Toni and his companion, Ernst Krebs, slid down

I

an ice slope some 1,600 feet in height. Krebs escaped with severe injuries, but Toni was killed.

The second ascent of the north face was made by two Munich climbers, J. Schmidbauer and T. Leiss, on July 15-19, 1935. They spent three days and two nights on the mountain. Five days later the famous Grindelwald guide, Hermann Steuri, and Dr Baur of Saxony, completed the ascent of the north face and the descent to the Hörnli hut in a single day, a brilliant achievement. They left the Hörnli hut at 12.45 a.m., and had reached the top of the slanting gully at 10 a.m. and the summit at 1.45 p.m. Only two *pitons* were used on the climb. They were back at the Hörnli hut early in the evening.

Herr Toni Hiebeler contributed to Signor Alfonso Bernardi's most useful anthology, *Il Gran Cervino*, an interesting summary of ascents of the north face up to 1961. In the thirty years after the first ascent the north face was climbed twenty-six times by an aggregate of seventy-four climbers—24 Austrians, 15 Swiss, 13 Germans, 5 Italians, 5 Poles, 3 British, 2 French, 2 Czechs, and presumably 5 others whose nationalities Herr Hiebeler does not give. The first, and so far only, solitary ascent was made in 1959 by the Austrian, Diether Machart, in the incredible time of five hours. Machart was killed three years later, in 1962, while attempting a solitary ascent of the Eiger Nordwand. The north face has so far claimed only one victim, Gustl Kröner, who was killed by falling stones at the beginning of the climb. Another Austrian, Leo Forstenlechner, climbed the north face with companions, and in the course of a later solitary attempt slid down the first ice slope but escaped without serious injury.

The first winter ascent of the north face is described in the next chapter.

CHAPTER XXI

The First Winter Ascent of
the North Face

Towards the end of June 1964 I spent two days at the Hotel Jungfrau, Wengernalp, with Kaspar von Almen, an expert mountaineer whose climbs include the famous north face of the Piz Badile, and Hilti von Allmen who was the first to climb the north face of the Matterhorn in winter. I had, of course, read his contribution to *The Mountain World* (1964) and the article which he wrote for *Il Gran Cervino*, but in the course of those days at Wengernalp I was able to satisfy my curiosity not only about the climb but also about the climber, and as this book will, I hope, be read not only by mountaineers but also by those who have never climbed, I did my best to elicit the facts which may perhaps help the non-mountaineering reader to appreciate the motive and general outlook of the greatest modern masters of a difficult and dangerous sport.

Hilti von Allmen's father was a teacher in a technical school for ornamental ironwork, particularly in connection with locks, when the second world war broke out. In the ensuing slump he lost his job and became a mechanic on the Mürren railway. From the first, Hilti von Allmen was interested in nothing but mountains. At the age of fifteen he climbed his first difficult peak, the Lobhorn, the base of which can be reached in a few hours from his home in Lauterbrunnen. This group of five rocky teeth is a magnificent training ground for a young mountaineer. I asked Hilti if his parents sympathized with his mountaineering ambitions. 'Not at all', he replied. 'My father's bad experiences in the war when he lost his job because of the crisis always influenced him. He had *die Krise in der Knochen* (the crisis in his bones).' He was determined that Hilti should have a job with an assured future. Hilti therefore was trained as a mechanic, but he hated the job.

'When I told my father that I wanted to be a ski-teacher in winter and a guide in summer, and chuck my job as a mechanic, he was not pleased. He thought that a ski-teacher's job was *nicht seriös*.[1] For him ski-teachers sit about in the bars and chase girls. But I became a ski-teacher all the same, and raced a little. I was never good enough for the Swiss "A" team, but I raced in the "B" team. In 1957 I went to England to learn the language, and in 1958 I became a guide.'

From the first Hilti specialized in the more difficult routes, the north faces of Piz Badile and Piz Roseg, many Dolomite climbs of extreme difficulty, the Mitteli ridge and the Lauper route on the Eiger. He climbed the notorious Eiger north face in a remarkably good time. He bivouaced at the beginning of the real difficulties, about three hours from the actual foot of the north face, and reached the summit next day. Among the last and greatest of the unsolved problems of the Alps were the north faces of the Matterhorn, Eiger and Grandes Jorasses, and it was inevitable that once these problems had been solved in summer, the mountaineering élite would be fascinated by the problem of making the first winter ascents. Shortly after Hiebeler and his companions had made the first winter ascent of the Eiger north face,[2] Walter Bonatti made the first attempt to climb the north face of the Matterhorn in winter.

Towards the end of December 1961 Hilti von Allmen and Paul Etter made their first attempt. In January 1962 an international party consisting of the Germans Hiebeler and Kinshofer, the Frenchman Mazeaud and the Austrian Krempke, had to abandon a gallant attempt on the third day, defeated by bad weather.

Paul Etter of Wallenstadt in the Canton of St Gall began life as an apprentice baker. Like Hilti, his one ambition was to climb,

[1] Literally 'not serious', *seriös* is untranslatable.
[2] The story of this climb has been told in *North Face in Winter* by Toni Hiebeler. English translation by Hugh Merrick.

and as he was not quite as strong as seemed desirable for severe climbs, he worked for some time as a miner to strengthen his muscles for serious mountaineering. He then obtained his certificate as a guide. Among the more brilliant of Paul Etter's climbs may be mentioned the north faces of the Piz Badile and Piz Roseg.

At the end of January 1962 von Allmen and Etter arrived in Zermatt and spent ten days in the Hörnli hut at the foot of the Matterhorn cliffs. Von Allmen was twenty-seven years old, Etter twenty-three. The weather was uncertain but the days of waiting were not wholly wasted. The normal hut temperature was minus 13 centigrade, and they soon discovered that bread and cheese when subjected to very low temperatures were frozen solid, so when they replenished their provisions at Zermatt they bought biscuits and chocolate and Bündnerfleisch (dried meat). Though snow fell during these days of waiting they were not unduly worried because they felt convinced that the prevailing west wind, blowing across the north face, would remove most of the loose snow.

Von Allmen and Etter were well aware of the fact that they were not unique in their ambition to make the first winter ascent of the north face of the Matterhorn, and they were therefore not particularly surprised when they were joined by two Austrians, Leo Schlömmer and Erick Krempke, four days before the attempt began, and on the eve of the attempt by three Germans who lived in Monaco, Werner Bittner, Peter Siegert and Rainer Kauschke. These three groups, in spite of the inevitable rivalry, felt, said von Allmen, 'as if in some strange way they were united by a kind of defensive alliance'.

On the night of February 2nd the Swiss Broadcasting Station predicted fine weather for February 3rd but uncertain weather on the 4th—not a very promising forecast for men who could not hope to complete their climb in one day. Nevertheless, all three groups decided to start. They left the Hörnli hut next morning at 2 a.m. The relations between these rival groups could not have been more cordial or more in conformity with the best traditions of the sport. It was decided that Hilti von Allmen and Paul Etter were probably faster than the other two groups and should therefore be the first to attack the face. All three parties kept together on the lower part of the climb, but it soon became apparent that von Allmen and Etter were the fastest of the three groups, and they accordingly separated.

For the benefit of the non-mountaineering reader let me briefly describe their equipment and technique. Many steep cliffs cannot be climbed without creating artificial footholds. *Pitons* are driven into the face of the cliff, and by a complicated rope technique the climber hoists himself from one artificial foothold to the next. Conservative climbers condemn what they call 'artificial climbing', but no mountaineer could possibly condemn the use of *pitons* for *security*. The leader drives a *piton* into ice or into a crack in the rock, and threads the rope between the leader and the next man through the ring of the *piton*. The illustration facing page 128, from a photograph by Hilti von Allmen, shows Paul Etter leading. Note the *piton* ring, the *piton* itself driven into a crack in the rock. If Etter had fallen, the fall would have been checked by the rope threaded through the *piton* ring. Note also the steel crampons which he is wearing on his boots. An expert can often dispense with the need to cut steps by driving these crampons into the ice.

The modern ice-axe is much shorter than the axes used by my generation. Like the old axe, it has a steel-pointed pick for cutting steps in ice, but the modern axe has a hammer instead of the broad edge which was used for hacking steps in hard snow. The hammer on the axe is used for hammering in *pitons*, but sometimes the axe has to be hammered into hard icy snow with the help of extra hammers. Von Allmen and Etter therefore both carried extra hammers. A felt boot worn inside the climbing boot helped to mitigate the effect of severe cold, and plastic helmets provided some slight protection against falling stones. The immense difficulties of the climb were aggravated by the fact that each climber had to carry a total weight of over fifteen kilograms (about thirty-two pounds).

The lowest third of the north face is ice, but the rest of the climb is an unattractive mixture of rocky slabs usually covered with pure ice or with ice with a top layer of snow. At 8 a.m. they had already reached a height of 12,487 feet (3,800 metres), and a little over 2,200 feet remained to be climbed, but the main difficulties of the ascent were concentrated into this upper section. The key to the north face is a broad cleft which begins at the base of the north face and ends a little below the level of the Swiss shoulder. The steep upward traverse to this broad cleft proved to be most difficult and perilous. They had to climb very steep rock slabs covered with about four inches of black ice. Had they tried to cut steps, this top layer of ice would almost certainly have peeled off, and consequently they had to climb on crampons. Owing to the steepness of the slope, about sixty-five degrees, they could only drive the front two spikes of their crampons into this shallow ice layer, and every movement was extremely delicate. On these ice-covered slabs they used special corkscrew *pitons*.

They had separated from the other parties at about 9.30 a.m., but from time to time the voices of the climbers below them, and the sound of hammering in of *pitons*, were carried up to them through the thin air. At 5 p.m. they began their anxious search for a ledge broad enough for a bivouac. Nowhere could they find a fairly level ledge about a square metre in area, but eventually they discovered a site just broad enough for their sleeping sacks, and they began the inevitable preparations, hammering in *pitons* to which the ropes round their bodies were to be attached during the night. It was during these preparations that a minor disaster occurred. Hilti dropped his crampons and they disappeared into the depths below unobserved by Etter who for the time being remained unaware of Hilti's lapse.

I asked Hilti what precautions they had taken to ensure help if they could neither complete the climb nor descend unassisted.

'There is a cleft which drops from the shoulder. We were confident that we could at least reach a point in this cleft not too far below the Swiss shoulder, and if we fired a red rocket, the Zermatt guides would have climbed to the shoulder and lowered enough rope to reach us.'

A 7 p.m. Etter fired the green rocket which signified that all was going well. From the valley, lights flickered up in reassuring response to their signals. Their friends had not forgotten them. Their radios were working, and they listened with anxiety to the forecast of west wind and snow, beginning in the afternoon. Far away in Lauterbrunnen, Hilti's parents listened to the weather

forecast with even greater anxiety, but heard with immense
relief that the green rocket had been fired.

Etter switched off the radio, and Hilti began to worry acutely
about the problem of completing the ascent without crampons.
In *The Mountain World* (1962-3)[1] von Allmen describes the
delicacy with which he broke the bad news to Paul Etter:

'I must tell Paul, and so I asked him casually what he would
do if he were at this point without crampons.

' "I'd climb on."

' "Really?"

' "Well, we have most of the traverses behind us, and on the
vertical pitches you could help me with a tight rope from above,
and it is not much further to the summit."

'Good old Paul! He swallowed hard and became as dumb as a
fish when he heard that it would be he who would have to pull
me up the next day.'

The ordeal of the wintry bivouac lasted fourteen hours, and
at approximately 7 a.m. they emerged reluctantly from the
comparative warmth of their sleeping sacks.

'Then came the first steps, without crampons . . . I noticed at
once that henceforward I would have to climb mainly with my
hands. I was not used to this, but it worked, for the distance
between us and the parties below continued to increase. We
climbed and climbed. When I followed, Paul always held the
rope taut, so that at the most I only occasionally slipped from a
foothold.'

One particularly difficult vertical pitch was only climbed by
hammering in three *pitons*. Fortunately this was the last serious
obstacle, for a wind was rising and it was through the first flakes
of a snowstorm that the summit Cross suddenly defined itself
against a grey sky. At 3.30 p.m. Hilti and Paul clasped hands on
the summit of one of the grimmest of Alpine cliffs.

'Shivering with excitement and cold, I tried to get out my
camera. Alas, the zipper was frozen shut—naturally! What's

[1] London, George Allen & Unwin.

more, my fingers were all stiff and refused to move. But at last I was able to click the shutter.

' "You'll need a plastic surgeon if you don't massage your nose at once", said Paul. We rubbed and rubbed, but my fingers remained stiff and without feeling. "We'll take care of both face and fingers in the Solvay hut." Time was pressing, for the weather was worsening. A little earlier we could still see down to Zermatt. Now we stood in driving snow. Inch-long beards of frozen snow grew all over our faces.

'I slid down more than I climbed, but Paul belayed. He would never lose his nerve. I knew that my fingers were no longer working and I climbed badly. I could not even grasp effectively the fixed ropes above the shoulder on the ridge. Here and there we stopped to shout to our comrades, who must be somewhere on the summit wall, for we could discover no traces of their having climbed out on to the shoulder. There was nothing to be seen. We shouted in vain. The storm tore the clouds to pieces on the ridge and thundered between the gendarmes and through the notches. It was as though express trains were constantly roaring past. "Go ahead, let yourself go, I'll hold you!" shouted Paul. Despite all our haste, there was no sign of the hut. I was tired and feared for my fingers, and I knew that we would have to bivouac once more.'

The snow on the rocks was deep enough to dig a hole, but the miseries of yet another bivouac in the open were aggravated for Hilti by the pain in his frost-bitten fingers. Their only luxury was some egg cognac which Paul's mother had brewed.

Suddenly they were buried in a snowslide. They struggled free, only to discover that they were bivouacing in the middle of a small chute. 'The same thing was repeated at regular intervals all through the night,' wrote Hilti, 'digging ourselves in, then a snowslide, then digging ourselves out to get some air, and then digging ourselves in again. It was just as well, for in this way we avoided becoming apathetic and we were protected at least a little from the storm.'

At 9.30 a.m. on February 5th they reached the Solvay hut. The snow had forced its way through every crack. It was impossible to open the inner door against which the snow had piled

up, and in order to force an entry into the hut, Hilti broke a
window and went through it head first into a snowdrift and
found himself below a snow-covered table. What little energy
they had left was spent in making the hut habitable. Their relief
in finding shelter was tempered by their acute anxiety about the
fate of the other climbers. They knew that their friends could
hardly have reached the summit before night fell, and would
almost certainly have been forced to bivouac for a second time
on the north face and to complete the climb in far worse conditions than those experienced by Hilti and Paul, who had reached
the summit before the weather deteriorated.

'Outside the hut,' writes Hilti von Allmen in his contribution
to *Il Gran Cervino*, 'the storm raged with a fury which showed
no sign of diminishing. We shouted again and again with all the
force of our lungs but in vain. We could do nothing but wait,
hope and pray, Paul particularly for he is a fervent Catholic,
that the five miserable climbers, lost in the hurricane, might
reach us in safety. I began to wonder whether the time had come
to fire a rocket as our agreed distress signal, but realized that the
rocket would not have been seen through the storm. Suddenly
at 9 p.m. the door was thrust open and the missing climbers
staggered in, masked in snow and ice. Indeed, they looked like
walking ice statues, but they were alive and uninjured.'

They had every reason to congratulate themselves. Hilti and
Paul had all but ceased to hope that all five climbers would complete the ascent of one of the most formidable of Alpine cliffs in
a storm and reach shelter alive. Towards noon on the following
day the storm relented, and the seven climbers began the descent
together, and were met while still on the rocks by friends who
had climbed up to meet them.

'In the twilight we reached the Hörnli hut. Champagne is
wonderful, but perhaps it was not the right thing for Paul, for
he had never touched it before. He thought it was apple cider
and was perplexed at his intoxication.'

I asked Hilti whether his father had been very proud of his
achievement.

'Yes, he was proud, but he did not see much sense in it.'

'My wife', I said, 'would agree with him'.

'Well, if you do not understand anything of what climbing means, it must seem stupid, but what I thought foolish was for Franz Schmid, who made the first ascent in summer of the north face, to say he could see no sense in our climb.'

And indeed the nuances which differentiate defensible and indefensible risks on these extreme climbs defy any attempt at rational classification.

'You see,' Hilti continued, 'I do not believe in taking risks. I was absolutely confident on that climb that each step could be secured. I am', he said with the utmost seriousness, 'a believer in the principle of "Safety First". I would not, for instance, jump over barbed wire, for I might catch my pants on it and fall.'

I heard next day of yet another distinguished exponent of Safety First mountaineering. I was having a drink with Mrs Fritz von Almen at the Scheidegg. She and her husband watched through telescopes the successful solitary ascent of the Eiger north face by Michel Darbellay of Verbier.

'We prepared a hot meal for him at 2 a.m., and I think he could certainly have reached the top that same day, for he climbed very fast, but it was very warm in the afternoon, and water was pouring down one crack which he had to climb, and so he thought it more prudent to wait. He told me he was a great believer in the principle of "Safety First".'

So am I, but my conception of safety priorities has more in common with Hilti's father's than with Hilti's.

Hilti had just passed his gliding test when we last met. 'I told my father I'd like to take him up as a passenger, but I'd have to complete thirty successful flights before getting a licence to carry a passenger.'

'Then I've still some time to live', said Hilti's father.

CHAPTER XXII

'Shadowy Personality'

During the months when I was at work on this book I found it easy to persuade myself that it was my duty to revisit my old friends the Sellas at Biella, and to spend some time at Breuil and at Zermatt. Duties may be divided into the pleasant and the unpleasant and no man has a greater devotion than I to pleasant duties. My host at Biella was the grandson of Quintino Sella, who financed the early Italian attempts on the Matterhorn.

The Monte Rosa was not open when we arrived at Zermatt so we stayed at the other Seiler hotel, the Mont Cervin, of which Herr Bernard Seiler, of the fourth generation, is the managing director. A sturdy representative of the fifth generation, Christopher, has already made his appearance.

I paid many visits to the famous Alpine museum, and I am deeply indebted to my friend Herr Karl Lehner, the Director of the Museum, not only for permission to reproduce some of his exhibits in this book but for all that I have learned from him not only on this but also on previous visits.

Herr Lehner, like every other member of an old Zermatt family, combines an immense admiration for Whymper's achievement with a very realistic judgment on Whymper as a man. 'He had only one real friend in Zermatt,' said Herr Lehner, 'my aunt, Tante Biner, who shaved him. Whenever Whymper returned to Zermatt he never failed to bring a little present for Tante Biner. From a journey to Italy, for instance, he brought back a little model of the Leaning Tower of Pisa.' A letter which Tante Biner wrote to Whymper is reproduced facing page 129 of this book.

I spent many happy hours, during this Zermatt visit, gossiping with my old friend Herr Bernard Biner. There is a delightful

140

sketch of Biner in Cicely Williams' *Zermatt Saga*, for Bernard in his day was a famous guide, and is also the son of a famous guide. He is a brilliant conversationalist and a master of four languages. He knew, of course, all the outstanding members of the Alpine Club who survived into his period, among them Sir Edward Davidson who, as we have seen, was responsible for the black-balling of Mummery on social grounds. Bernard Biner said something which implied that Davidson's own social position was insecure.

'One day at the Riffelalp,' Biner said, 'my father was talking to Davidson and a friend of his, and a very aristocratic English clergyman, the Reverend Gordon, who was also a great scholar, passed into the hotel. A little later, when my father came into the hotel, the Reverend Gordon told him that he ought really not to mix "*mit diesen fetten gewöhnliche Menschen die um ihre Fleischtöpfe sitzen*" (with these fat vulgar men who sit round their fleshpots).'[1]

Biner's grandmother had a small hotel, and one day Whymper walked in and ordered lunch with champagne for himself and three friends and walked out without even offering to pay. At that time Whymper was publishing new editions at regular intervals of his *Guide to Zermatt* for which he collected advertisements. He indicated by stars the hotels of which he approved, and he acted on the assumption that every hotelier would be genuinely honoured by his presence as an uninvited guest at a meal, or at least deem it imprudent to present him with a bill.

'Nobody in the valley', said Bernard Biner, 'liked Whymper, and even those who didn't like Taugwalder thought that Whymper's attack on him really wicked. You remember that Whymper has some long story about how the Taugwalders asked him to write in their Führerbuch that they had not been paid so that people would feel sympathetic . . . '

'Yes, I've dealt with that in a chapter which I've just written.'

'Well the only language which old Taugwalder could really speak well is our own Zermatt dialect, and the only language in

[1] *Exodus* xii.3.

which Whymper could carry on a real conversation was English. And even if they had been able to speak easily to each other, this particular conversation is incredible.

'Taugwalder had an unhappy time after the accident. Many guides were jealous of his success in making the first ascent of the Matterhorn and some of them were really unpleasant about him. There were one or two disagreeable incidents. And then he drank a little too much and was criticized on that account by serious people. All of which explains why he emigrated to America.'

'Karl Lehner', I remarked, 'told me that his emigration had no connection with the accident. It was a time when a lot of Swiss were suddenly attracted by the idea of emigrating.'

'I don't agree', said Biner. 'It was partly at least due to the unpleasant atmosphere for which the accident was responsible.'

'What interests me', I said, 'about the attitude of the Zermatters to Whymper is that I have met nobody who admired him as a man but there seems to be a great admiration for his achievement.'

'Well, why not?', said Biner. 'Toni Sailer, who won three gold medals at the Cortina Olympics, is a very nice man, but if he was as nasty as Whymper he would still have won three gold medals, and whatever Whymper may have done in the valley he was the first up the Matterhorn. And you must remember that for us *Berglers* the tourist is always right. An American recently claimed that he had climbed the Matterhorn in record time. Yes, a record for a tourist. One of our Zermatters had been up in a shorter time, but you don't suppose, do you, that he would publish the fact?'

Biner mentioned the case of a new route claimed by an amateur which a guide had previously climbed on his variant of a busman's holiday, but kept quiet about. And of course Biner was right. Alfred Wills, on his return to Grindelwald from what he firmly believed to be the first ascent of the Wetterhorn, was feted by the villagers, many of whom knew that one of Wills' guides had himself already been up the Wetterhorn twice.[1]

There will be nothing insincere in the official tributes which

---

[1] *A Century of Mountaineering*, p. 36.

will undoubtedly be paid to Whymper during the centenary celebrations of 1965 for these will be tributes not to his personal character, but to his achievement both as a mountaineer and as the author of an Alpine classic. It would however be fatuous for even the most fervent admirer of *Scrambles amongst the Alps* to claim that its author should be immune from criticism as a man, particularly in view of the fact that Whymper never hesitated to criticise other people and was wholly reckless in publishing the vilest accusations against the Taugwalders, accusations which have been rejected as utterly unfounded by all who have written books or articles about the Matterhorn. It would be equally fatuous to belittle Whymper's achievements because of the more distasteful aspects of his eccentric personality.

In the course of our last day at Zermatt we visited the Monte Rosa hotel, which was just about to open and which, in spite of modern improvements, remains in essentials substantially unchanged since Whymper's day. I first stopped at the Monte Rosa after climbing the Matterhorn in 1907, and I can still remember the awe with which I watched members of the Alpine Club taking their places at the table traditionally reserved for the Club.

There are acrobatic climbers for whom real mountaineering only began with the invention of *pitons*, and for such philistines the Monte Rosa may be nothing more than a hotel, but for civilized mountaineers the Monte Rosa is also a shrine, dedicated to the memory of the Early Fathers of the Mountain Faith.

As we entered the Monte Rosa I remembered Whymper's return from the Matterhorn and Seiler following him in silence to his room and asking 'What is the matter?' and Whymper's reply 'The Taugwalders and I have returned'.

The Palace Hotel, Mürren, has associations with the beginnings of Alpine ski-racing even closer than those of the Monte Rosa with mountaineering, for it was in Room 4 of the Palace that the first rules for Downhill and Slalom Racing were formulated and the Kandahar Ski Club founded, but no skier will ever enter Room 4 with feelings comparable to those with which a mountaineer first enters the Monte Rosa. Why is this? Partly because there are some for whom mountaineering is not only a sport. The history of mountaineering has indeed some faint analogies with the rise of a new religious movement, for many a climber who has lost all contact with institutional religion has attempted to find compensation in mountain worship.

'If I were to invent a new idolatry,' wrote Leslie Stephen, who left the Church in which he had been ordained to write *An Agnostic's Apology*, 'I should prostrate myself not before bird or beast or ocean but before one of those mighty masses to which, in spite of all reason, it is impossible not to attribute some shadowy personality.'

'Shadowy personality' or, perhaps, the shadow of a Personality, the great Architect who has created the mountains for our delight, an arena of splendid adventure in our youth, and a treasure house of memory in the evening of our lives. There is no peak to which it is easier, 'in spite of all reason', to attribute a shadowy personality than the superb mountain of immortal memories which is the glory of Zermatt and of the Valtournanche.

POSTSCRIPT

The Matterhorn was the scene of a fantastic achievement in 1965, the year in which the centenary of the first ascent was celebrated. The famous Italian mountaineer, Walter Bonatti, made a solitary ascent of the north face by the most direct route, arriving on the summit on Monday, February 22nd, at 3.30 p.m. He spent an aggregate of ninety-four hours on the wall. During the three nights the temperature sometimes sank to minus 30 degrees C. It was so cold that he never slept. He had a very heavy sack, which he would attach by a rope to a *piton* while he climbed the next section, driving in *pitons*. He would then lower himself by a rope attached to a *piton*, collect the sack, and reclimb the section, removing the *pitons* as he climbed. In effect he thus climbed the north wall twice.

He was photographed by pilots who flew as near him as they could. Hermann Geiger piloted Bonatti's wife, Bianca, who watched her husband climb the last few metres to the summit.

Bonatti has fantastic power of enduring great cold. On most of the climb he dispensed with gloves, for gloves of course aggravate the difficulties of a very severe climb with very scanty handholds.